HISTORY OF SANTA MONICA

Stories

HiStory of Santa Monica

Stories

By Michael J. Atwood

Aqueous Books

Published by Aqueous Books
P.O. Box 12784
Pensacola, FL 32591

www.aqueousbooks.com

Published in the United States of America

ISBN: 978-0-9826734-0-9

First Aqueous Books printing, 2010

Cover art and design: Lisa Graves Design

To my wife, Melanie—for your love and patience

To William and Megan

To the loving memory of my mother

And the living spirit of my father

I am still living with your ghost
Lonely and dreaming of the West Coast
— Everclear, "Santa Monica"

Gazing up into the darkness I saw myself as a creature driven
and derided by vanity; and my eyes burned with anguish and anger.
— James Joyce, "Araby"

Author's Note

While writing this collection, I've asked much of my family and friends, who have taken the time to read, edit, and comment on these stories. It is with sincere appreciation that I thank them for doing so. *HiStory of Santa Monica* travels between the vastly distinct settings of California and Boston, where most of my friends and family reside. Their opinions about literary elements such as setting, use of vernacular, and actual history were essential. Without their assistance and interest, this collection could not have come to fruition.

It is with extreme gratitude that I acknowledge the friendship, mentorship, and editorial collaboration of Mr. Eric Wasserman. Eric and I met in a fiction workshop at Emerson College in 2001, while he was completing his MFA and a manuscript that eventually would become *The Temporary Life*. At the time, I was preparing to apply for a Master of Professional Writing at the University of Southern California and entered the class quite blindly, but was taken under the wing of this seasoned fiction writer. Later, we spent time living in Santa Monica, where stories from this collection and my son, William, were born. Eric's influence on my fiction can be found in the most successful and recognized stories of the collection; his persistence directly contributed to my completion of this work. I'd also like to thank his wife, Thea, for her unending support with the editing of my writing— particularly my thesis from USC, as well as serving as the Web master of mjatwood.com.

The education I received at Boston College and USC also greatly influenced this collection. Special thanks to my high school journalism and English teachers, John Conceison and Christopher Servant, respectively, who shaped my writing while at Bishop Feehan High School. To my undergraduate English professors, Laura Tanner, John Doherty, and Robert Wallace, who taught me how to analyze and write about literature. To *Boston Globe* sports editor, Larry Ames—thank you for the opportunity to write about high school sports in your legendary department. To my professors at USC: Susan Compo, Syd Field, Shelley Berman, Donald Freed, and James Ragan—thanks for helping take my writing to a higher level. To George Wendt—your friendship and editorial advice were tremendously encouraging. To Jason Vittorini—thanks for your encouragement in Santa Monica to perform comedy and write fiction. To Brian Frates—thanks for just listening and reading these tales when I needed an opinion. To my editor, John Andre, at the *North Attleborough Free Press*—thanks for giving me an opportunity to express my opinion and work on my craft each week. Special thanks to Mike Heppner and Erin McKnight—your editing brought the collection to a new level. To Lisa Graves—your countless hours on the book jacket went beyond all my expectations. Thanks again to Gloria Mindock—the first editor of fiction to recognize my ability to write and publish my work. And finally, heartfelt thanks to Cynthia Reeser and Aqueous Books for having faith in this collection and making it their very first publication.

CONTENTS

HiStory of Santa Monica

ANCIENT HIBERNIANS

As I glance through the windshield of my parents' used silver Grand Marquis, I suddenly realize that everything in nature is temporary. The foliage along Route 6 in western Rhode Island—once green and vibrant—is now dying. A sudden wave of panic runs through me as I study the red and orange sunburst leaves. I grasp the wheel a bit tighter and steady the used car as it crosses the Connecticut state line. It's a Friday afternoon in November and my mother, father, and I are on the way to my uncle's funeral.

It is no secret that my father has never purchased a new car. There have been several vehicles in my lifetime: a '79 cardinal-red Pontiac Bonneville; an '88 sky-blue V-6 Oldsmobile; a '91 black Cadillac El Dorado with a sunroof; and even an '83 wood-paneled Chevy Caprice wagon with a rebuilt V-8 engine and reinforced steel hitch that pulled our family trailer to Maine each summer. All of these cars are dead now, covered in rust in a forgotten junkyard somewhere outside of Providence. But, here I am again, driving another used vehicle doomed to suffer the same fate. I just pray that it won't happen on this trip.

● ● ●

I despise these used cars because of the inconvenience they've caused me. There were the breakdowns and the flat tires. There were nights on the roadside waiting for AAA to come. There were the unbearable phone calls to my father, who decided that I had made the rusty muffler fall off or the battery die. There were missed dates with pretty girls and unattended parties in high school. I often fantasize about the day when I can walk into a car dealership in Los Angeles and buy myself a new luxury automobile.

When my parents picked me up at Logan Airport in Boston this morning, my father proudly leaned against this glistening silver Grand Marquis like a hunter posing with his captured game. He'd wiped down the hood with his best handkerchief and related how he'd shopped around carefully until he found something with low mileage, good tires, a limited warranty, power windows, and interior climate control. The dashboard, he said, even has a state-of-the-art stereo system so he can play his Irish folk music or listen to Red Sox games.

"It's got these new speakers," my father brags. "They told me that the sub-woofer gives the bodhran a booming resonation. My Irish music never sounded so brilliant."

The car, my father continues, is part of that used-car salesman's myth: *The Florida Car*. The kind of car owned by an old, retired schoolteacher who keeps it in The South for the winter, only drives it a mile to church and back on Sundays during the spring and summer, and never takes it out in the rain.

"These new cars they're making," my father growls from the passenger seat, "depreciate as soon as you drive 'em off the lot. Too fancy."

And now, here I am, at the wheel of this new car, traveling for two hours on a frigid day to Hartford, Connecticut. I'm 3,000 miles from my apartment complex in California, where I left sunny skies and a 70-degree temperature. I couldn't believe it when my dad asked me to drive his new-used car. At first I wanted to believe it was a gesture that I am now an adult, but because he won't stop talking I know something's wrong. He's the opposite of my mother. When she's upset she never says a word. He keeps squinting and rubbing his knee, and I know that something isn't right.

* * *

"Personally, I enjoy taking these back roads," my father says, dabbing his bald scalp with a handkerchief stitched with his initials—a Christmas gift from my sister, part of a set. "Better than those clogged-up interstates, you know?"

Where I live in Los Angeles, I am surrounded by cement. It is a city that doesn't offer any surreptitious routes like this one, although I try desperately to find them. Instead, I am forced to take the freeways: the 405 and the 101 always packed with traffic, always making me late for a show or audition. Sometimes the traffic and heat are so bad, you want to kill yourself. However, in New England, there is a sense of freedom on these former horse trails that once propelled Indian tribes, militia, and presidential carriages toward New York or Boston. These roads will always be here; short-cuts, according to my father.

I notice him leaning down to massage his knee—again.

"What did you do to your leg?" I finally inquire.

"Nothing," he mutters. "Just a cramp."

"He hurt it falling down the stairs," chimes in my mother from the backseat, in-between puffs off her long Salem Light and work on her Dell crossword puzzle. It's the first thing she's said since they picked me up at Logan, when she inquired who dropped me off at LAX, hoping it was a girlfriend. When I told her it was my friend, Theo Schwartzman, she asked me, "What is he?" I reminded her that he is a professor of creative writing at Santa Monica College, and she corrected me by saying, "No, I mean, what *is* he? That sounds like a Jewish name. I didn't know you have Jewish friends, now. Aren't there any Catholic boys in L.A.?"

I look into the rearview mirror and study her skinny face, aged and pale, the cigarette dangling from her lips as she speaks.

"He fell because he lost his balance and slipped halfway down," she whispers through a cloud of smoke.

"Now, that's a bunch of bullshit," my father shoots back. He turns to me. "I just twisted on some ice on the back walk during the first snowstorm."

"You gotta be careful, Dad," I begin.

* * *

17

"Don't tell me about coordination, Fella!" he retorts. "You had two left feet until you were fourteen."

"His eyes are going, too," says my mother over my shoulder. "He can hardly see out of his left one. I think it's the cataracts. That's why he got into the car accident."

"Car accident?" I gasp. "What car accident?"

"Maybe you better cut down on the Chesterfields, Lady, and stop blowing smoke out of the proverbial flutter valve," my father says angrily, turning and pointing at her as if she's a temperamental child.

He turns to me and thumbs backwards.

"She's gotta quit those cancer sticks. Are you still smoking?"

"No," I insist. "I quit six months ago. But you have to put salt on that walk when there's ice."

My father's round face turns red with frustration.

"Keep your eyes on the damn road and mind your own business," he says, leaning toward the odometer. "How fast are you going, anyway?"

"Thirty-five," I respond.

"Too damn fast. Slow down."

"Don't worry, Gabriel," jabs my mother again. "He can't see the numbers anyway, just like he couldn't see that guy passing him on the left when he took off his mirror."

I gently release the accelerator and shake my head, trying to block out the ensuing argument. I crack the window, letting the cold air in to relieve myself of the secondhand smoke.

It has been three years since I moved to California to become a comedian, much to my parents' chagrin. I'd taught junior high school just outside of Boston for awhile after college, but felt paralyzed. I wanted to pursue my creative ambitions.

"Teaching is a good job. Reliable," my father had stated many times. "You show me another profession that gives you that kind of time off. Pursue your funny business during July and August."

* * *

When I decided to put in my letter of resignation and bought a plane ticket to Los Angeles, my father tried to talk me out of the move.

"Why do you want to live in California?" he scoffed, as I shared a cigarette with my mother at the bus station.

"Frank, leave him alone. He's made up his mind," she said, resigned.

"They're soft out there. No work ethic. No rituals or religion. No sense of family," he continued.

Still, I bid them farewell. There was no looking back in my mind; I was going to Hollywood and starting a new life. I swore that the money I'd make would prevent me from living the life that my parents had: one of used cars and two-week vacations.

But lately, I'm starting to believe the joke is on me. Comedy in L.A. is a few nights a week— open mics in the back of Chinese and Mexican restaurants. Gigs at the Comedy Store or the Improv are hard to come by, unless they pick your name out of a hat on Tuesday nights, and I've blown much of what I had in the bank after cashing in my Massachusetts state teaching retirement fund. My father would kill me if he knew I had done that. I will take the source of the other money to the grave—the money that had arrived in a discreet envelope just last month. To add to my disappointment, I was called back for this funeral with nothing to show for my time away: no stories of success, no friendships with stars—nothing. In many ways, I'm ashamed. I am the prodigal son returning home.

As the ride continues, I imagine that the oversized Grand Marquis, I'm driving, is a hearse. I adjust the mirror and stare back at my mother, who is now asleep, looking as if she is dead. The skinniness of her face is apparent—her cheekbones protruding in a way that I haven't noticed before. My father leans back and closes his eyes for a few minutes, too. His red face worries me— diabetes, heart trouble, hypertension—maybe all of them. It seems they've aged so much since I've left home. I wonder when I'll be flying back for their funerals.

My eyes focus back on the road as a blur of orange catches my attention. It is a construction crew—a team of four workers taking their time to patch up a small stretch of torn-up tar and macadam stone before the winter moves in. In L.A., this would be a Hispanic team plugging away in the hot sun, but here it is a bunch of white working stiffs, shivering in the cold, staring back at me as if to say, "I wish I studied harder in school." I jam on the brakes then maneuver past them carefully, moving across the double-yellow lines. As I catch the eye of the worker holding a sign that reads *Caution*, I suddenly feel ashamed.

"Get around 'em," my father commands, awakened by the commotion. "Watch that pothole. Stay out of trouble. Careful, careful now."

My mother leans forward and puts her bony hand on my shoulder. She's awake again.

"Nice and easy, Gabriel," she says. "We're not going to be late for the wake. We have plenty of time."

But for my Uncle James, time has run out. Eight years of prostate cancer, which he fought bravely up until the last months. He'd dropped fifty pounds and his skin had turned from pale to jaundiced. Our family is kind in times of sickness, trying to stay optimistic, saying things like how much he looked like his father near the end. But the reality was that he was dying. The chemotherapy had deprived him of his masculinity. To make matters worse, the cancer had gotten into his bones. In just a few months, he was gone.

Despite these images of his demise, I'm craving a cigarette. I feel the pack hidden inside my jacket but shake off the thought. That damn billboard back on Santa Monica Boulevard, the one that posts the current deaths due to smoking for the year, serves as my conscience.

"Your mother smokes in my new car. The whole goddamned interior is ruined," my father complains. "It's killing this beautiful vehicle! Thank Jesus she doesn't smoke in that expensive Volvo your sister bought."

"Where is she, anyway?" I ask.

"She's meeting us there," my mother replies, as she cracks her window and tosses a cigarette out. "She had an ultrasound at Beth Israel."

"So, how much you making as a comedian?" my father inquires.

"Not much," I admit.

"When are they gonna pay you?" he continues.

"First of all, who's 'they'?" I ask. "And second, I get paid when I write or say something that can be sold."

"Maybe this Schwartzman fellow knows somebody who can pay you for your jokes."

"Dad, he's a professor."

"But he's a Jew, right? He has to know people in your industry. The Jews run Hollywood," says my father. "You're the wrong religion. Better convert. Change your name. I can't think of any successful Catholic comedians besides George Carlin."

"Isn't that a bit anti-Semitic, Dad?"

"It's true, Gabriel," my mother chimes in. "The Jews have run the movie business since the beginning. Comedy, too: Marty Feldman, Shelley Berman, Jerry Seinfeld, Sid Caesar, George Burns."

"Don't forget Bob Newhart," my dad adds. "I actually always liked Newhart."

"I don't think he's Jewish, Dad."

My father waves me off and looks at the radio hungrily.

"You wanna turn on the game?" he asks.

"No," I say bluntly.

He grimaces and flips it on anyway to a static-filled radio station with announcers discussing the line-up for tonight's Celtics game. I wonder how much longer we have left on this journey.

*

When we arrive at the Best Western in Hartford it is dark. I drop my parents off at the lobby entrance and swing the car around the back. I'm thinking how my father would have taken up two spaces to make sure that no one could open their door and damage the paint on his "beautiful" new-used car. I rest my head on the wheel, unsure if it is jet lag or pure exhaustion from the anxious ride with my aging parents. I get out and find another Camel Light, wondering if the bar is similar to the one in the Best Western in Beverly Hills, where I perform my stand-up routine on Thursday nights.

As I smoke alone in the parking lot, I admit to myself that my Uncle James was probably the only one in my family who actually supported my move out West. I recall how I met him for lunch at The Black Rose in Boston, where he claimed the Guinness tasted as good as the pints he'd had in Dublin. Lunch was always our special godfather and godson tradition when I was a kid, only then it was milkshakes and burgers at McDonald's. But as I got older, it became trips to Red Sox games and a few beers.

"Don't tell your dad that I'm here to celebrate," he had instructed with a grin. "He wants me to talk you out of this."

"It'll be our little secret. I'll take it to the grave," I promised.

We sat and talked about family and life over a lunch of bangers and mash and cabbage. After dinner was finished, we started on pints of Guinness.

"You have to follow your dreams," Uncle James had stated after our third beer. "I've got grandkids, a beautiful family. A life only a king could dream of. But if I was to die tomorrow, I'd give it all away to do what you're doing."

I nodded but didn't truly believe the words coming from my uncle's mouth.

"Come on, Uncle Jimmy," I said. "You've made it. Your family is your legacy."

"No, no. It's true. Hell, I waited until I was retired to get on a plane and fly to Ireland, even though I wanted to go when I was younger," he continued. "I've been going twice a year just to catch up. Your view of things changes when a doctor tells you in some cramped examination room that you're on your way out. All that's left is a bunch of regrets, Lad."

"Don't say that, Uncle Jimmy."

My uncle smiled, then leaned over to ruffle my hair. It made me feel like I was six again.

"Listen," he said. "What's that line I like? The one from *The Great Gatsby*? Come on, Teach, you know."

I shook my head. "I don't know. I haven't read it in a while."

* * *

My uncle closed his eyes to try to recall. "Let us celebrate a man while he's still alive, not after he's dead," he said. "Wolfsheim, the Jew mobster, said that. I've been going back and reading the classics. And I'm going to confession again."

He smiled, then his hand went into his jacket and he took out an envelope. I cringed as he slid it across the table.

"A little something to help you get started," he said. "Just until you're as big as Seinfeld."

I shook my head.

"Take it," he insisted. "You'll do the same one day when you have a special nephew of your own and are asked to be his godfather."

That was the last time I saw my Uncle James. I remember the color in his face, the life still in him. And now, I would see his pale, lifeless body in a casket of my "twin uncle," as my mother called him.

I finish my cigarette in the darkened parking lot and walk slowly to the lobby of the Best Western, feeling a little depressed. I start looking for the bar but my parents are waiting and I feel guilty about wanting a drink, so we slowly make our way up to the room on the second floor. I set my bags on the straps of the luggage holders and look around, my eyes fixating on the bed. I grimace. There is only one.

"We can order a cot," my mother says. "I told the desk clerk two double-beds, not one king-size. He was apparently too busy surfing the Internet on his iPod."

"Ah…he can sleep on the floor. It's good for the back. Save us some money," my father chimes in.

My mother ignores him and moves to the phone, picks it up, and dials the front desk. My father walks up behind her, speaking over her shoulder.

"Tell them we're not paying extra," he exclaims. "These hotels, they'll rob you blind. Remember the one on the Cape last anniversary?"

I depart for the bathroom, strip down and run the water until steam rises, then shower for a good ten minutes. I get out, towel off, shave my stubble, and put on a pressed shirt and my dark

Brooks Brothers suit, then comb my mop-like hair as I stare into the mirror. I button up the jacket, straighten my red tie, and exit the bathroom. My father, now shirtless with his hairy chest and round belly hanging out, turns and studies me, curious.

"Three buttons. Fancy," he remarks. "Didn't realize we had Harry Hollywood with us over here, Honey."

He's right. It's a very sharp English-cut suit, a purchase that was funded by the envelope from Uncle James. I'd worn it to audition for a game show and then an open call for the *Tonight Show*, but was not selected. I remember standing outside the studio in Burbank in 90-degree heat, trying not to sweat as I studied the smirking comedians in jeans and T-shirts. Still, I want to look good for the wake. It makes me feel important, as if things have gone differently for me. There will be relatives there whom I haven't seen in years, ones who never fully understood my exile to Hollywood. Even if it isn't true, I need to look successful. I have long imagined wearing the suit to pick up my parents from LAX after getting my first big break, but they have never once shown any interest in visiting Los Angeles. My father even goes so far as to use the excuse that my mother is afraid of flying.

In the small hotel room, I watch my mother get ready and study her thinning frame as she walks around in her white slip, another long Salem Light dangling from her mouth. She has aged over the last few years and looks even older in the bright light of the room. I feel a gnawing in my stomach over the fact that neither of my parents has been to the doctor since the Kennedy administration. I grab the remote and turn to CNN in hopes of some distraction, but it's just a report on a sniper, who is still wandering the countryside picking off victims. More death. I wipe some lint off my dark suit and announce that I am going to get the car.

"No smoking out there, Harry Hollywood," my father shouts as the hotel door slams behind me.

*

We arrive at McLean's Funeral Home in East Hartford around eight, and I drop my parents off at the front and park the Grand Marquis next to a long black hearse. I walk slowly up the steps and feel the surge of heat as I enter the home. For the first time all day, I feel warm and relaxed.

I catch a glimpse of my cousins and aunt standing in a line by the casket. Five boys and one girl, the men all with salt-and-pepper beards, looking like noblemen or princes out of some Shakespearean production. But they also look tired.

I turn to a collage of photos laid out of my uncle, my godfather. Some are old, black-and-white shots of a skinny, dark-haired young man playing basketball, and there is another of him walking down the aisle with the aunt my father never liked, then one with my grandfather and his eldest son at a graduation. My favorite is one taken in the '70s; Uncle James is laughing, a gap in the center of his teeth, a cigarette in one hand, and a can of Bud in the other.

Then, there's a transformation in the color photos to a distinguished gray-haired man with his grandchildren, playing cards, another of him traveling through Ireland for the first time. I know I will not see the same man lying in the wood casket up front, and that scares me.

I walk past my father, who is loudly discussing the Notre Dame-BC match-up this weekend and how his cousin, the famous attorney, wouldn't be coming, since he had traveled out to South Bend for the game and the plans couldn't be changed. "They're wearing green this weekend instead of blue," he shouts at the priest, who is inches away from him. "Every nine years a miracle happens for BC. Flutie's Hail Mary in '84 and Gordon's kick in '93. Could be a big one for them this year, Father."

I swerve around the priest, afraid he might ask me if I attend St. Monica's each Sunday, if I go to confession, if I'm still a good altar boy.

My sister taps me on the shoulder and I turn and look down at her stomach. It seems that she is always pregnant at funerals. "It's good that you've come all this way," she says. "Mom must be happy."

She's expecting her fifth child in December, probably another girl (to my father's dismay). She's alone; her four kids are back at the hotel with her husband. My parents used to tell me to get married and have a nice family like my sister, but they've given up all hope of that idea. I don't even tell them about the pretty girl Schwartzman introduced me to on a blind date the other week that I'd like to see again, an Irish-Catholic girl from Studio City.

After a moment, my sister and I approach the casket. She takes my arm as we kneel and pray.

His face is gaunt and sunken, his cheekbones pushing up the jaundiced skin that even make-up can't disguise. We stare stoically but I am in disbelief at what the disease has done to him, wasting him down to skin and bones. I turn my eyes away and, instead, try to focus on the silver Celtic cross leaning on his shoulder and think about the good times. We stand slowly and bless ourselves, moving to the condolence line, shaking hands with my cousins and expressing our sadness. I answer a few questions about California and try to relate how great it is, but stop short on elaboration because I feel guilty about taking the focus away from my Uncle James. For a moment, I have a yearning to run from the line and return to the sun's warmth.

Instead, my sister and I sit in some folding chairs in the back of the room and catch up. She says she's doing well, living in Belmont, driving the new Volvo, and enjoying her married life and her girls. She's nervous about the impending birth of her fifth child, but mentions that she's also closing a real estate deal on Monday so she hopes she doesn't go into labor early. Then, she quietly asks if I need money. I whisper to her that "I'm okay," since I feel guilty about the money.

I still owe her.

With all these debts—these family loans—I feel like a degenerate gambler. I force a smile and she smiles back. That's when I notice a man who has just entered the room. He is wearing a blue-strapped medal around his neck.

"Did this guy run the Boston Marathon?" I ask, nodding to the medal-draped man.

My sister shrugs and we watch him console my aunt and cousins. For a moment, he somehow gets caught by my father in a loud conversation about college football. More men begin to arrive with medals, eight in all, very somber, in dark suits and green ties. As they look up to the casket, the priest steps to the front of the room and announces that there will be a prayer ceremony, tells us to gather round.

* * *

I watch as the eight men move deeper into the room and line up near the casket in orderly military fashion. I wonder if they've drilled for hours to perform this ritual. I look again to my sister, notice her strawberry-blonde hair is longer than the last time I saw her.

"Who are these guys?" I whisper, offended. "Should they be here?"

She grins and shrugs again, just as confused as I am. A short, gray-haired man who appears to be the leader of the crew steps forward and takes out a piece of paper, his hands shaking.

"Brother James Dugan Bradley was a member of our organization for over thirty years. We, the Ancient Order of Hibernians of East Hartford, Connecticut, would like to express our sincere condolences to Mrs. Mary Margaret Bradley for the passing of her beloved husband, as well as to the children, grandchildren, siblings, and friends of this generous and loving man."

He nods to my father and my aunt, his hands still quivering as he looks out to the crowd. Another man steps forward and breaks the awkward silence.

"Our Father…"

We transition into spontaneous prayer: Hail Marys, Our Fathers, more Hail Marys, a few Blessed Bes to the Fathers, Sons, and Holy Ghosts. Then, as quickly as they arrived, the men with the medals march out, back to their Hibernian camp to train for another wake, play some cards, sing Irish songs, and drink beer.

"What the hell was that?" I ask my sister.

"I didn't even know he was a member of anything other than his church and that bowling team," she replies. She kisses me on the cheek and says calmly, "It's really good to see you here, Gabriel. I've missed seeing you." She pats her stomach. "By the way, I think this one will be a boy. It just feels different. And, we want to know…would you be his godfather?"

"I'm a poor comic," I say, trying to laugh. "I'm no godfather."

"Well," she says, "it will be a good excuse to come back home. You could do all those godfather and godson things that I was always so jealous Uncle James did with you. Anyway, just think about it."

I kiss her on the cheek, get up, walk out to the front of the funeral home, distracted but amused by the little Hibernian escapade, and move into the parking lot. I take out my Camels and pack them tight. I put one in my mouth and click my lighter, but feel a presence beside me.

"What are you doing?" asks a little boy's voice.

I turn to see my cousin's youngest, James III, standing on the front steps, aloof. He is in his tan parka. I quickly remove my cigarette, then smile at him.

"Nothing," I reply. "I was just hot in there."

"I thought you lived in California. That's what Grandpa told me. Isn't it hot there?" he asks.

"Yeah. I guess I'm a little sad that your grandpa is in heaven."

"No, he's not," says little James.

"Sure, sure, he is," I reply, saying what I think is the right thing, what Uncle James would want me to say. "He's with Jesus now." I pause awkwardly. "Why are you out here, James?"

I wonder if he's been out, trying to avoid the open casket. He shrugs at me and watches the Ancient Hibernians get into their silver Toyota minivan.

"You see those guys?" I ask, pointing to the men.

He slowly opens his jacket to reveal a blue-and-gold medal. I nod and look at it.

"They gave me Grandpa's medal," he says, turning the piece around to reveal *James Dugan Bradley* engraved on the back. It seems to sparkle in the light, and I lean forward and ruffle his hair.

"Grandpa's in my heart," he finally tells me.

I look at him and smile. We turn and watch as the Ancient Hibernians peel out of the parking lot, playing "Danny Boy" on their radio. The driver gives me a tip of his tam o'shanter as he passes.

"Mine, too," I say softly.

I begin to feel the cold coming down upon me, and wonder how many hours I have before I fly back to California.

* * *

THE OLD APARTMENT

I went back to Santa Monica last week. I snapped photos and walked underneath the shade of the palm trees in Palisades Park. It felt pretty good. I took time to look out at the pier and then turned and stared up the coast, north toward Malibu, at the half-moon-shaped shoreline that extends like a bent arm into the sea. I studied the waves of the Pacific—it was all very beautiful, something right out of a dream, some kind of paradise. Nothing could go wrong here, I thought. Nothing.

I was experiencing a day, one that included all of the things I had neglected to do when I lived here, when we were busy with life's interruptions.

But, upon my return, I felt like a Spanish explorer discovering the place for the first time. I had read several books on the history of Santa Monica and it's said that Gaspar de Portola was among the first white Europeans who marched his men down what is now Wilshire Boulevard and set eyes on the coastal cove. What a feeling he must've had in his chest looking down at the unadulterated sea before him. He must have thought he had discovered Eden.

* * *

I paused for another moment and admired the pious-looking concrete statue of St. Monica near Ocean Boulevard—the ivory-colored one that overlooks the trash-strewn dirt path where a homeless man lay asleep on a tarp that matched the color of the ocean. Joggers passed unaware and tourists stood snapping photos of the motionless Ferris wheel on the pier, illuminated and spinning in the morning sun. I didn't blame them for not noticing the homeless man; that Ferris wheel was mesmerizing and reminded me of the one sometimes used on the cover of *The Great Gatsby*—the jacket that features Coney Island and depicts Daisy Buchanan's face mystically hovering behind it. Who could resist such a colorful landmark? It made the filth and disease seem irrelevant.

I once read that Santa Monica was named for the dripping springs discovered by the Spaniards who, inspired by their Catholicism, immediately associated the water with the tears Monica shed for her son Augustine's sins before he reformed. I often wonder if my mother shed the same tears for my misdoings.

After a few quiet moments, I left the ocean behind, continuing east down California Avenue, to St. Monica's Church, a shrine surrounded by high-rise condos and expensive townhomes. I entered the old church, walked in, knelt, and said a prayer. I lit a candle in the cool darkness of the silent, vacant chapel. I recalled that, despite the proximity to our old apartment, we hadn't come here much, and I didn't really know why that was—I couldn't put my finger on it. As I emerged from the church, the bright morning light beat down upon me and I felt ashamed of the things I'd neglected to do in my life. Maybe that was why I had decided to accept my company's offer to take this trip.

I wandered back down to 3rd Street Promenade and went into the old Barnes & Noble bookstore on the corner of Wilshire, the one with three levels, a Starbucks, an escalator. It still had a great fiction section, the one where, on separate occasions, I saw Sugar Ray Leonard and Michael Crichton browsing the aisles. There had been a Borders on The Promenade, but a bad lease and unstable economic times had shut it down. I bought some postcards to mail to friends and family back East to prove where I was. After, I wandered back into the 70-degree winter air and sat beside the stone fountain outside the Banana Republic. I imagined it was snowing back home.

* * *

What I recall most about my visit was that I found myself looking at things—closely, almost studying them in the manner my father might study a new-used car before he purchased the vehicle. I felt I was a detective trying to solve a mystery—someone investigating a missing person's case. You see, I'd lost something in Santa Monica. Or maybe I had just left something behind. I had moved back to the East three years before and, on this day, Santa Monica seemed in many ways exactly the same— just as I remembered, as if things had not moved forward. Even the owner of my old liquor store, Sam, looked identical and immediately remembered me from daily visits to purchase beer and cigarettes. Nothing had changed—except me.

I was three years older, six years older than when I first arrived in California. My hair was salt-and-pepper and my beard primarily salt. I had a master's degree, two kids, a mortgage on my childhood house, two used Volvos, thirteen years of professional experience in the insurance business under my belt, and more importantly, I carried twenty pounds less. I didn't buy cigarettes anymore and I drank less coffee; I stuck to two beers instead of ten.

As I came out of the liquor store and pulled my black suitcase past the dry cleaners and El Cholo that border Wilshire, I came to 11th Street, the location of my old apartment. I studied the white exterior and the large numerals, "1157," on the façade. It was in this apartment that my son was conceived and later brought home to; the place he will always call his first residence. It was here that a homeless woman lived on my doorstep for many years and once tried to kick down the sectioned glass door. It was here that I shared building space with a female comedian, a massage therapist who disappeared to Colorado for months at a time, a Goth bartender, and an aspiring actor who drove a black '69 Chevy and, I always suspected, carried a gun. It was here that we were sandwiched between a dive bar called J.P.'s and a foreign automotive garage where the owner would have a fit if you parked in front of his chained-in driveway at night. It was here that we paid $800 a month to Topa Properties, who leased a large building with its name on the side in Century City off Santa Monica Boulevard, just past the billboard that listed the number of deaths from smoking per year. It was here at this old apartment that I hoped they wouldn't find out we had moved in under my brother-in-law's rent-controlled lease. It was here that I left a piece of me.

* * *

The old apartment was a place where I studied for hours while my wife went to her Catholic school job. It was the place where I started my daily runs up to San Vicente as I trained for my first marathon during the winter months when back in Boston it was snowing. It was the place where my son would always be from, whether he liked it or not. It was here that 10,000 other children had been diagnosed.

*

I had made the decision to visit the old apartment just after Christmas—to take a look at where it had all happened. I was a fraud investigator for a large insurance company out of Boston, and travel had brought me to the West Coast. There were a series of boring seminars at my conference in San Diego that made me want to go back to my room at the Hotel del Coronado for a nap, thinking that maybe I was sleeping in one of the rooms Marilyn Monroe had been in when she was filming *Some Like It Hot*. After two days of enduring the redundancies, I just checked out. I went directly to the train station and bought a ticket for the two o'clock, and took the Sea Coaster up north to see some friends in Los Angeles. The ride on the Coaster is scenic, one of the best coastal train rides in the United States. I had my usual distractions: iPhone and laptop—I sent my wife a message that everything was going well. I was on my own for the first time in a while.

That evening, I'd met up with my college roommate and we drank and laughed and recalled times when we were single and without the complication of kids. I slept like a dead man at his home in Brentwood, just around the corner from the O.J. Simpson murders, and then in the pre-dawn hours, I quietly departed. Later, I bought a hot drink from the Coffee Bean on Wilshire and 9th, and walked the two blocks down to the old apartment.

In many ways, it looked the same: the old, white exterior covered with black residue from pollution and car exhaust. The landlord had installed a wooden gate in to keep intruders out. I wished I had thought of a barrier like that.

The old apartment was where my son lived for two years. Where he was subject to the noise of the constant traffic on Wilshire, the exhaust from idling vehicles at nearby traffic lights and the adjacent foreign-motor garage. There in his crib, he was vulnerable to the vulgarity of the drunks from J.P.'s, the wireless signals and cellular phones that sent their currencies through our walls, along with all the sinister elements that an urban environment fosters.

And I had done nothing.

I looked over the gate at the dusty steps by the stoop where I'd smoke Camels whose smoke infiltrated the tears in the screen in the old door we'd never fixed.

As I moved away from the gate and headed west, it occurred to me that I was walking in circles. But there was one last visit I needed to make. It wasn't medical. But it was.

I needed to get it straight in my head that it wasn't me who'd caused this. I'd conducted a little investigation on the culprit; however, just because you can get answers doesn't always mean you can also get reparation.

I stood outside the medical building, studying it. I remembered the view from the examining room on the fifth floor—you could see all the way to the ocean. It was a glorious panorama in a small space where something hideous took place.

I began researching vaccines as soon as my son was diagnosed—that's just what parents do when they find out. There had always been talk about it, but here's the thing—we had left the scene of the crime before we could get the answers we needed. The offense had been committed—maybe quite unknowingly—by a nurse dressed in pink medical scrubs who had inserted the syringe needle into my son's arm.

There was terrible sickness after the booster shots. There was regression, loss of speech, and that same lethargic look, as if a lobotomy had been performed. He was not the same boy that went home to the old apartment.

*

Medical fraud was a big part of my caseload. Individuals sometimes made outrageous claims against doctors and ran up insurance costs because they wanted an easy settlement for missed diagnoses or alleged diseases. But I was there to stop it. I made my living preventing things.

I finally put out my cigarette—my first one in a while—and entered the building, pulling my black suitcase behind me. I thought about my son back home in Boston. I thought about the life expectancy of male smokers being three-and-a-half-years shorter than non-smokers: I could make it to seventy-eight. I thought of the syringe going into my son. It was a crime that I intended to uncover. I could not blame the old apartment, the chemicals in my cigarette smoke, the number of times he'd bumped his skull against the coffee table—or the time I'd dropped him in the snow when we were back East on a visit. It was the fault of medicine, the judgment of a doctor who had not thought to investigate a cerebral vulnerability. He was to blame, a doctor who went home to his palatial manor tucked in the canyon between here and the Palisades, his black Mercedes sitting in the driveway, his weekends spent at the Jonathon Club or on his yacht aimed toward Catalina. On this day, all debts would be settled.

As I entered the office, I did not know what I was going to do. Vengeance is a strange emotion, and retribution reveals its face in many different forms. In my business, however, punishment came mostly with litigation. I'd delivered more lawsuits to people by passing them on to my legal counsel at the company with my findings. I'd read Dr. Ethan Starkfield's research on the MMR vaccine thoroughly, and I felt it was true, or at least it was what I wanted, what I needed, to hear. He was the voice that I, and many other parents, desired in a time of darkness.

The friendly receptionist looked up at me, but I didn't smile back. For a moment, I turned and looked out the fifth-floor window and tried to catch a glimpse of the old apartment. I could see St. Monica's rising through the verdant trees of the neighborhood. I slowly reached into my black suitcase, turned back, and forced a smile.

"Is the doctor in?"

WINDMILLS

It is a Saturday morning, two days before Christmas, and we are driving to Palm Springs to buy a house. There are windmills spinning alongside this desert highway. They are tall, white, and mechanical, resembling 3,000 skinny children twirling in unison on a playground. I stare through my dirty windshield across the desert floor, over the sand and tumbleweeds, at the spiraling ivory towers of steel. For a moment, I have the sensation that we are completely still, frozen by some kind of magnetic force emanating from the mysterious structures. I quickly glance at the speedometer of my used Volvo, which reads seventy-five miles per hour, and realize it is an error of my perception.

I look into the rearview mirror at my sleeping son, who would love the oscillating pinwheels in the morning zephyr, but decide not to disturb his slumber. I glance over at my wife and consider shaking her from sleep, but I've become wise in my six months as a father; I let her continue her much-needed nap since she was up with the baby most of the night. I am left to enjoy the landscape by myself.

* * *

Odd things appear in the desert. Last summer, I made the solitary drive in this ten-year-old Volvo across the Mojave to Las Vegas on the I-15. At one point, I saw stones sailing across the playa near Death Valley. Several miles ahead, I witnessed an abandoned car burning on the side of the road. I slowed down and for a moment stared into the fire, but saw no sign of life. When I rolled down my window, I felt the oppressive heat against my pale face and wondered whether if I stayed long enough I would melt like a wax doll. After a moment, I rolled up my window and continued, praying that I would make it to civilization before something bad happened. I wondered if someone was inside that burning automobile, or if it was the act of an arsonist who lurked along the highway.

I stopped for gas and a burger at a roadside diner before heading back down the road. I looked in my rearview mirror for the smoke from the car I had passed. I had a feeling in my chest that someone was following me. Then, just outside Las Vegas around dusk, a pack of coyotes wandered across the highway and blocked my path. I stopped the car and sat anxiously as they surrounded me. One paused and stared at me with rapid yellow eyes, opening his mouth to reveal sharp teeth. I revved my engine, accelerated through the pack, and sped off toward the City of Sin.

I've never told anyone about these events—not even my wife—because I am unsure of their factuality.

Life often works this way: you witness something unfathomable, but there is no one there to attest that it is true; fear sends you away with no evidence.

However, as we pass these windmills, I realize that their giant turbines are indeed real. They stand in contrast with the dark, snow-capped San Bernardino Mountains hovering in the background. And since we left the darkness of Santa Monica, they are the first truly engaging landmark. Their rotors gyrate slowly, sending invisible electricity out to the air conditioners of the desert communities that loom ahead in the Coachella Valley, just a few miles beyond this San Gorgonio Pass. I recall the outcry back home that came with the construction of just one windmill on the South Shore, and Ted Kennedy's plea to stop a huge turbine being built in Chatham because he thought it would destroy the maritime landscape (not to mention the value of some of the family's real estate holdings). Here, in the middle of nowhere, stand 3,000 windmills bothering no one.

* * *

I turn my eyes back to the road and click on the static-filled radio, anxious for the Palm Springs freeway exit. I want to get off this long desert highway; I am tired from a grueling school week. An old Beach Boys' tune finally comes on and Mike Love sings, *Christmas comes this time of year*, as I steer toward the off-ramp, wondering why we've driven so far from the ocean and why I am in California for Christmas instead of my parents' snow-filled backyard in Massachusetts. It suddenly occurs to me that we may have just arrived in our new hometown.

*

I've contemplated the idea of my son growing up in the desert—about what kind of life I could offer him. His pale complexion is better suited for New England, but the homes here are cheaper. There would be plenty of recreation: the tennis and golf are the very best in the world, home to major international tournaments. But still, I question sometimes if we are making too much of buying a house. I know we can't go on living in a cramped apartment with a crying baby, but I wonder if these California badlands offer a solution in the form of desert exile. Hollywood is a long way from here.

I remember the house I grew up in, in Rhode Island. It was a small ranch in a bedroom community close to Providence, which was literally tucked inside the armpit of Massachusetts. There was nothing extraordinary about the house. It was my parents' first purchase, all they could afford with a new baby on the way. It was quaint, two bedrooms, attached garage set at the end of a cul-de-sac, surrounded by woods abutting the Catholic nursing home, the Hospice of St. Brigid, which was home to my invalid grandmother for her final, isolated years.

We've looked at just about every house and condo in West Los Angeles. They have all been expensive, two bedrooms, and span from the coast out to Culver City. We've even gone down to Playa Del Rey and Westchester and walked through the complexes built on methane fields or wetlands, ones that overlook the cement aqueduct of the Los Angeles River or the runways of LAX. They are almost double what we can afford as teachers.

There are days when I'll step out into the sun on my cement stoop in Santa Monica and wonder if my son will be forced to grow up in an apartment, a consequence of my quixotic dreams of show business. No matter what time of day, the drunks from the bar next-door are usually there, high on cheap cannabis and beer. I wonder if they came to California years ago with the same ambitions and, when those dissipated, they found solace in barroom billiards and whiskey. I am looking for a solution in the desert—a means to keep us in California for a few more years—maybe for the rest of our lives. We can't just give up and move home; there is too much at stake. We are looking at forgotten land to prevent us from abandoning our dream.

The house shopping began as soon as my wife fell pregnant. I had returned from my Uncle James's funeral in Connecticut and met her on a blind date in Studio City. We eloped soon after and were married in Cabo San Lucas. We had no intention of starting a family at that time; we just did. And with our new family, it only made sense to take the next step.

I look over as my wife wakes up and rubs her eyes.

"Where are we?" she asks with a yawn.

"We're here," I reply. "In the desert."

I pull onto Frank Sinatra Drive. They say Ol' Blue Eyes lived in a gated compound just down the road in Rancho Mirage. I wonder if he came here, as I do, haunted by visions of his boyhood back East; if he felt a sense of betrayal for missing those New Jersey winters. I read that Frank liked it because people left him alone. That sounds appealing to me.

I turn onto Palm Canyon Drive and study the Spanish architecture that blends with glass window shops. There are Christmas trees with red ribbons and ornaments, along with yuletide decorations suspended along the boulevard. Palm trees and sequoias bend over the avenue and red-and-white flowers adorn the grassy median, fake reindeers standing in the pastoral landscape.

"Looks like Beverly Hills," I comment. "Except in the desert."

"It's nice," she continues, studying the shops on El Paseo.

"Don't get any ideas," I remind her. "We're broke."

"I can't window-shop?" she asks innocently.

* * *

"Give me your credit cards," I respond.

I pull the car off Palm Canyon into a parking structure and get out and stretch. A Bing Crosby tune is playing in the courtyard. I hear the sound of a fountain below us and for a brief moment feel like having a cigarette, but I quit six months ago as a promise to my wife.

The ride from L.A. to Palm Springs seems as if it always takes two hours. The trip back, however, is unpredictable. There's the end-of-weekend traffic, no different from the mass exodus from Cape Cod on warm Sunday nights in the summer. I remember those rides, the feeling of the wind blowing in through the back window of our station wagon as my father listened to the Red Sox game. We've journeyed out here before during our three years in California but this is our first time with the baby, so any ideas of a romantic weekend have slipped away. I take my son out of his car seat as my wife unfolds the stroller. I buckle him in and we walk down the entrance ramp to the sidewalk.

The weather is pleasant, a bit warmer than the 60 degrees in Santa Monica, where the ocean brings fog and wind on occasion. I know that this mild temperature is short-lived, for in four months the 70 degrees will rise close to well over 100.

"I'm hungry," my wife says. "Let's get some Mexican food before we meet the Realtor...what's his name?"

"Mori Wasserman," I say.

"Is he the broker?"

"Broker, owner, agent, everything," I say. "I think old Mori's been in the business a while."

"What business is that, exactly?" my wife asks pessimistically.

"The one that's going to get you your dream house," I shoot back.

I push my son along the hot sidewalk as he looks around at all the interesting colors and buildings, studying them. Santa Claus is ringing a bell outside the Brooks Brothers store and my son giggles as Santa waves to us. In the desert heat, I suddenly imagine myself in the cold parking lot of a shopping mall in Rhode Island, holding my mother's hand with my right and my Christmas list with my left.

* * *

We continue past Santa and I reflect on our real estate search. We started by signing up for e-mail listings, hoping to find a condo near our rent-controlled apartment that would fit into our tight budget. After my wife became pregnant, I quickly took a job at a local Catholic high school. It paid the rent, but now we needed to pool our income to pay a mortgage.

Then I found the answer. I was sitting in The Coffee Bean on Wilshire one Saturday morning typing a screenplay on my laptop, when through the large glass window I saw a man standing on the corner wearing a sign that announced: *Homes in the desert, just an hour from Los Angeles!* I stood up to take a closer look at the advertisement. *Realize your American Dream. Homes starting in the high $200,000s.*

I sprinted out into traffic toward the man. This was the answer! A home just outside of Los Angeles, a mere hour away. It was too good to be true. We could own a house and be a short drive from the city. As I approached the unshaven man wearing the Dodgers cap, he backed away.

"I ain't got any money, Buddy," he insisted.

"I don't want your money," I assured him. "How do I get one of those houses?"

He looked at me oddly and smiled as I pointed at his sign. It was as if I was the first person to actually acknowledge the advertisement. He reached into his pocket and handed me a card.

"Call this '800' number," he said. "Ask for Mori. He'll set you up real good."

"Thanks," I said. "You Mori's partner?"

"Nah," he said. "Just an employee out of his satellite office."

And now, here we are a month later, enjoying our burritos and margaritas at Taco Del Deserto, thumbing through local real estate guides. My son happily devours his bottled formula and Cheerios. I want to give him spicy rice, salsa, and black beans, but he's only six months old and my wife insists on a strict diet.

"I like this one," she says. "And it's on a golf course."

I look at the picture and nod. I have to admit that the prospect of country club living seems appealing.

"Very nice," I say. "But we don't have that much."

* * *

"But there's a community pool," she says, sliding the listing to me.

"Too much," I reply.

"Well, how much do we have?"

"Not that much," I say. "We're teachers."

I think about my job. My contract was negotiated over a few pints with a priest named Father Seamus Porter. We settled around one in the morning, when the bar was closing.

"Jesus will take care of the rest," he assured me with a Guinness in his hand. "He's taken care of me for fifty years, Gabriel. All the way from Cork."

I nodded.

"And Jesus brought you to Pacific Palisades, Father?" I joked.

"God is good," he replied, taking a swig of his beer.

"I have a son now, Father," I reminded him. "We'd like to buy a house."

"The doors to the house of God are always open," he said. "And we'll also need your services as the volunteer basketball coach. Be patient."

"Easy for you to say with that free house next door to the campus," I replied.

"Again, God is good!"

But God wasn't that good to me. My assignment was a Catholic junior high class full of stress. After the first month of school, my mother dropped dead of an aneurysm and I had to fly back to Boston. I returned to Santa Monica and staggered around between a phase of depression and drunkenness. I started smoking heavily and my wife threatened to take my son and walk away. To make matters worse, Father Porter was named in a sexual abuse case that shook up the entire parish. Hollywood reporters were following me around for a comment since I had been named the interim assistant principal. In the end, we decided that a move to the desert might be the best scenario, and here we are, about to be exiled to the land of sand for the sins of a priest.

After the Mexican meal, I wander out to the courtyard in front of the Spanish fountain and call Mori, the head of Desert Oasis Resort Properties, Inc. He tells me that he's running a few minutes late and to meet him at the first property, near Dean Martin Way, just past Jerry Lewis Avenue. It's a bank-owned property, he relates, a "short sale" they are eager to get an offer on. I hang up and think about my sister doing her last-minute Christmas shopping for us before she goes to the FedEx store to mail the packages to our doorstep. I call my friend, Schwartzman, and ask if he can stop by and pick up the presents before the homeless folks or a coyote can get at them. He asks if I'll be back for New Year's Eve and if I want to go to Hollywood to a new bar called Magnolia near Sunset and Vine. I look at my wife laughing with my son by the fountain and tell him probably not. Besides, Schwartzman's wife, Dea, is still sore at me for breaking up with a friend of hers just before Easter last year.

We drive the ten minutes to our potential new house. It's nice, better than anything we've seen in Los Angeles. I stretch as Mori Wasserman's big black Cadillac pulls up to the curb. He gets out: sky-blue suit, Western bolo tie, and white leather boots that click on the pavement.

"Gabriel Bradley, I presume," he says with a New York accent. "Morris T. Wasserman, Desert Oasis Resort Properties, Incorporated."

He shakes my hand and pats my son's head.

"Oh, my goodness. A new child! *Mazel tov!*" says Mori. "And nonetheless, a masculine child!"

"Thanks," I reply, shooting my wife a smirk.

"Let's give the missus a look at this desert estate, shall we?"

My wife smiles. I am not as totally enamored, and hold my son tight in my arms as Mori takes her hand and leads her into the desert bungalow.

Inside, Mori gives us the tour. It's obvious the place needs work, but according to Mori the home is perfect. I feel myself sinking, realizing we're being taken for a ride by 'Ol Mori.

"And out back, there's a nice little yard for little Ian," he says.

"His name is Liam," I say in an annoyed tone.

"Yeah, yeah, right. Liam," he laughs, as he slides the glass door to reveal a small in-ground pool and a patch of grass.

"Not much to mow," says Mori. "But the entertaining you could do here, I'll tell you."

I look at the structure and notice some cracks in the exterior.

"Any earthquakes out here, Mori?"

* * *

46

He taps his chin.

"Let's see, the wife and I moved here in '76," he begins. "I'd say we've had a handful…4.2 in April…but for the most part, there's not much….unless you take the missus dancing." He leans in and gives my flattered wife a hug at her hip. "Your insurance will take care of anything unexpected."

"Well," I say. "We appreciate your time. But we don't like anything unexpected."

A strange look comes over Mori's face, and he stares at me oddly.

"You don't like this palatial manor, Gabe?" he asks.

"It's Gabriel," I correct him. "And no, I don't think this one is for us."

He frowns and looks at my wife.

"Well, what does the missus think?"

My wife looks at me, knowing I'm going to kill her if she disagrees, but it is too late. Mori and this desert home have won her heart.

"I like it," she says defiantly. "I want to live here. It's great."

Mori claps his hands and lets out a hoot. My son thinks this is hilarious and begins to laugh. My face turns beet-red and suddenly I hate the desert.

"Well, then, all that's left to do is go back to my office and sign the papers. It's air-conditioned. We'll send your offer right along," Mori says gleefully. "The bank will be thrilled."

He turns and leads my wife back through the sliding glass doors into the kitchen for one more look. I follow angrily with my son. I put him back in his stroller and look at my arms that are red from holding him so tightly. As our real estate agent points out the window treatments to my wife, I know that there's only one solution to our problem. I smile and walk behind.

"Mori, are these cornices?" I ask bitterly, pointing to the green-striped boxes above the window.

He turns and looks at me.

"Umm…well, I'm not quite sure what you'd call them," he says.

My wife looks at me disdainfully. She knows I'm stealing from a show I saw on the Home Network.

* * *

47

"What's the problem?" I ask. "We practically own the place. Right, Mori?"

Mori looks at me weakly as my son tries to climb up the table leg.

"We might want to watch the scratches," he says. "We'll talk more at my office after I make a phone call. Follow me back."

We follow Mori's black Cadillac to Frank Sinatra Boulevard, and then back toward Rancho Mirage. My wife is steaming angry with me as she sits, arms folded. She knows now that I won't sign anything, that my heart is back East, and that her California dreams will be short-lived.

Silence.

"You're right," I finally say, softly.

"What?" she screams. "What did you say?"

"I haven't been doing my job," I say. "As a father and a husband. I apologize."

"What? What do you mean?" she demands.

I look ahead at Mori's slow-moving Cadillac and can almost feel his eyes upon mine, staring in the rearview mirror, just waiting for me to try and get away.

"What I mean is that I need to look out for both of you, more often. Do what's right for us."

My wife looks at me suspiciously as Mori slowly goes through a yellow light, his left hand out the driver's window waving for me to follow through. But I have a six-month-old baby in the back, so I begin to slow the Volvo. The signal turns red as Mori fills the middle of the intersection, and that's when a silver Lexus slams right into his Cadillac. The sound of crunching metal and breaking glass lasts an instant, until everything goes still and my son begins to cry from the backseat. My wife immediately turns to see if Liam is okay as I watch Mori move his car slowly off the main road, toward the opposite side of the intersection. Then, my wife snaps back and stares at me—cold.

I throw up my hands. "I swear that wasn't my fault," I say. She folds her arms and looks out her window.

I notice a sign for the Palm Springs Airport and hastily click on my right-hand blinker. The word *escape* rings in my head. My wife starts to say something and I gently reach out and put my hand on her thigh. Her eyes begin to well up with tiny lakes and when the green light appears, I turn the Volvo toward the highway as the alternator begins to rattle underneath the hood.

*

We are driving home and the windmills rise up in front of the San Gorgonio Pass. I look back at my son and once again, he is asleep. I pull the car to the side of road, angry with myself, and pause for a moment. My wife opens her reddened eyes and looks at me.

"What's wrong?" she asks. "Why are we stopping here?"

The road behind us is dark and quiet. I look in my rearview mirror but see only a long empty path of tar leading back through the desert to Palm Springs—our promised land. It's illuminated by the orange sun, which is burning out brilliantly in the occident. There are no cars leaving. It's Christmas Eve in California and I feel a yearning once again for the East—for home. I hesitantly open my car door and walk across the dusty desert floor to the other side of the Volvo. As I stand there—for a moment—I feel like a cowboy.

I open the door and take my son in my arms, holding him tight as if I will never let him go. He awakes and looks at me curiously, then out to the giant spinning windmills strung with Christmas lights, which begin to flicker on.

"What on earth are you doing?" my wife demands from inside the car.

"Shhh," I whisper. "This is nice. I want him to see it."

"See what, Gabriel?"

"His Christmas gift," I say. I kiss my son's forehead as his eyes widen, and we begin to walk slowly toward the windmills.

SHEBEEN

Mick, the bartender, was literally run off his feet. He ignored the aching legs that seemed to be betraying him, and leaned his dishwater-cracked hands against the hard oak bar—struggling to read the lips of another fervent patron over the noise of Irish folk music permeating the pub. On the cramped stage in front of the bar was a four-piece session band, led by a stout, red-faced singer lamenting "The Troubles" in Ireland. For some reason, on this night, in the darkness of this Santa Monica shebeen, Mick felt no empathy for or allegiance to any cause. His mind was elsewhere.

It was the annual Ancient Hibernians dinner—the third year of the clandestine affair, kept secret due to Prohibition. Still, every Irishman from Los Angeles to Pasadena knew about it and was sure to stroll through the back banquet room of McLean's Hotel and collect a plate of corned beef and cabbage to eat with their pint of dark stout. It occurred to Mick that it was quite odd to be celebrating St. Patrick's Day in California. However, business was good and a card game was forming in the back room amidst a cloud of cigar smoke. The local police force had been well compensated, as was the staff at McLean's. Mick was a loyal servant to his boss, Jimmy, the head of the McLean gang that had

* * *

51

come west from Boston. He looked beneath the bar at the bucket full of cash by the revolver he wondered if he would ever have to use.

Mick translated the patron's order, *Pionta Guinness, le do thoil*—"A pint of Guinness, please." As if driven by a motor, he reached down, grabbed yet another pint glass, and then shifted the tap downward to pour the beer. He set the glass down and let the creamy foam settle, then wiped his hands with the damp bar towel, tossing it into a sink filled with gray water. He felt like a priest offering sacred drink to his sinful customers, listening to their confessions behind his wooden façade. They were here for a charitable cause—to give money back to the Irish and to support a movement that was about to infiltrate Los Angeles politics and society. Mick found it ironic that the rent went back to a Jew landlord who sat waiting in the desert.

The patron eagerly picked up his pint, offered a "cheers" in Gaelic, and Mick returned the man an almost religious nod and accepted the currency from the damp oak bar. He watched the man disappear into the crowd as if being swallowed by the ocean eleven streets away. Mick stared into the crowd, enveloped in cigarette smoke, and felt the bodhran beat against his chest.

There was a feeling within him lately—a strange anxiety—that he was not unfamiliar with; it was a deep, derided desire to escape. As a devout Catholic, prayer had solved his questions of loyalty and faith in the past. But, lately, for some reason, he had felt like such a fraud. He was Irish—his parents had emigrated from County Wexford to Boston almost thirty years prior. However, here at McLean's Hotel, his mock accent, and all the rest of it, was as phony as any movie being filmed ten miles down the road in Hollywood.

Mick adjusted his suspenders underneath his kelly-green vest and felt that reoccurring twinge in his stomach.

*

It was the same sensation he'd felt waking up on Christmas Day in Santa Monica the first year he'd moved here from Boston. He recalled listening to his son laugh on his wife's lap as they ripped open their presents, while Bessie Smith sang the blues on their oversized Philco radio box. He'd smiled as he watched from the windowsill of their cramped flat. 70 degrees and sunny on Christmas Day, Mick thought—what would his mother think?

The Mass they'd attended at St. Monica's was offered by a Jesuit who had lived in Mexico and spoke of the poverty he'd seen on his mission. He'd even ended the Mass by shifting from Latin to Spanish, signaling to those who had immigrated to Los Angles and now lived in the Chavez Ravine slums.

Mick looked down upon Wilshire Boulevard, watching motorcars pass and the palm trees sway in the wind as he smoked his twelve-cent Camels. A palm leaf fell to the sidewalk and blew onto the street. He watched as a Ford drove over it.

The boulevard had changed so much in their three years—it had become busy, and the trolley to Hollywood rattled past as it did until early evening; there were more newcomers every day. The population of Santa Monica had grown by 10,000 people, according to a story in the previous week's *Times*, since they'd moved here in 1925. He looked across at a real estate office and a bank on the corner of 11th Street. There had been an orange grove there before tractors cleared the property. The owner, a wealthy Jew named Lankstein, had bought it from a farmer and pasted his name on the front, almost as a sign of defiance to the anti-Semitic sentiments in the neighborhood. Mick didn't mind the Jew's ambition or the fact that he tried to compete with his shy business—it was the fact that he'd used his money and leverage to take down the citrus orchard. Mick had enjoyed looking out at the orange trees in the morning while he drank his coffee.

He let the sash fall away, darkening the room, and turned back and studied his growing family in front of the Christmas tree. It just didn't make sense to live like this; there was a second baby on the way.

His wife, Shannon, held up the cocktail dress he'd bought her with his bar earnings.

"Oh, Mick—it's beautiful," she said, sucking in her pregnant stomach and modeling the dress on her otherwise slim body. "Do I look like Greta Garbo?"

"Absolutely," he said, moving to their wet bar, pouring a second martini and sipping it. He made another for his wife and handed it to her with a kiss on the lips. She was quite beautiful, still, he thought. Shannon had red hair, a thin frame, and mesmerizing emerald green eyes. She had grown up around the corner from him in Dorchester and was his friend Mangan's older sister. He'd loved her practically his whole life, since he had watched her from behind the sash of his parents' second-floor window as a boy.

"Cigarette?" he asked her.

She nodded and he slipped one between her lips, then lit it from his matchbook advertising the new hotel, Casa Del Mar, down south of the pier near Main Street.

He stood, took a sip of his own drink, and winced. He hated gin, but it was Christmas—and it was in vogue. He'd have a few stouts later, down at the pub, but for now he would try to accommodate his wife's taste.

Shannon had taken to the fact that there was money to spend. In Boston, they had lived on the second floor of his parents' row house on Sullivan Street. Mick had randomly bumped into Jimmy on a Sunday night after Mass at a secret shebeen in the back of Dugan's house on Savin Hill. He had been back in the neighborhood recruiting bar workers and an accord was reached—Jimmy wanted to surround himself with loyal Irishmen from the neighborhood. Mick had realized something very early on: loyalty would keep him and his family safe in Los Angeles. With the offer came two train tickets: a small investment for Jimmy, since McLean's had been robbed blind by local workers in its first few months in business. When that happened there was blood, and blood was expensive for a new operation in a new town.

A Louis Armstrong number came on and Mick set the drink down and tickled his son, Liam, to a floor covered in red-and-green wrapping paper. Times were good. Mick knew that if he moved up in the order with the McLean gang, he'd have a bungalow closer to the shore by the following Christmas. There were opportunities within the organization, ones that would establish him once and for all. He thought of his parents back in Dorchester, probably freezing, and the letters from his father saying he could move back and join the pipe fitter's union.

But Mick had other plans.

*

The three months since Christmas had gone by in the snap of a finger. The winter had been beautiful—70 degrees every day, and his wife had pushed the pram around with the kids while he'd slept a few hours after his shifts.

He turned toward the entrance to the shebeen, noticing his friend, Gabriel Bradley, talking to Jimmy, and hoped he wasn't getting involved—his nature was too good for this lifestyle. Gabriel was a writer and a Catholic schoolteacher—one of his closest friends in Los Angeles. He, too, had grown up in the neighborhood back in Dorchester, but attended the Latin school instead of the Jesuit school that Mick and Jimmy had gone to. Just two weeks before, Gabriel received a Western Union telegram announcing that his brother, Patrick, had washed up on a beach off Quincy Bay. The funeral had since been held, and Mick had consoled him. Gabriel was now looking for a new purpose.

He'd invited Gabriel to dinner at his apartment after Mass the previous Sunday, and Shannon had cooked a nice meal for them. Then, after the children were asleep, they had walked to Third Street to the cinema to watch a flicker called *The Racket* and talked about movie ideas that would make them rich. His friend was a great storyteller and orator—Mick wondered if he would make a move into local politics one day.

They were all, in their own way, trying to preserve something that their parents would be proud of. But there was also money to be made and as he accepted the patrons' greenbacks, Mick cleared the rest of the scattered bills from the counter and threw dollars and a few coins into his bucket, then turned and discreetly poured himself a shot of warm whiskey. They had Jameson but he wished for a Bushmills, the top-shelf stuff Jimmy kept in the back.

Mick looked at the clock; it was nearly eight. Jimmy had many balls in the air, including some real estate prospecting in the Palisades, a rural section of forgotten land where Will Rogers had built a mansion with polo fields nearby. With the explosion of the population over the last few years, 1928

* * *

had been a fine year. He looked down to a copy of *Saturday Evening Post* and studied the picture of the new Ford sedan he was going to buy this week from a dealer in Culver City—$800 seemed like a lot, but he had made some deliveries for Jimmy. In California, it was important to have a good motorcar, one that allowed you to take the windshield down and soak up the sun. He thought about driving up the coast with his family toward Malibu in his new car, perhaps after work with Gabriel, cruising down Sunset toward Hollywood and Vine. He'd come here with hope that he could eventually work in the pictures. Instead, he focused on his family. He would keep this job and see what panned out.

Jimmy came over and studied him at the bar with a grimace.

"Put it away," he said firmly, nodding to the magazine. "And no drinkin' off the till. You're acting like a member of the Gustin Gang, for Christ's sake. We're not common, petty thieves, you know."

"Sorry," said Mick.

"We've got customers; there's plenty to be made tonight. And keep up the accent," he said with a smirk. "Folks out here fancy it. They're not coming in for the service—they want liquor, music, cards, and women."

"Yes," Mick replied.

They'd known each other back in Boston. Both of them had gone to the Jesuit secondary school downtown before the priests had bought land in Newton and turned it into a college. Jimmy had been a good athlete and had gotten offers to go play baseball in college. But he had followed Joe Kennedy's lead on a tip he'd received—Mick wondered if he was funded by the entrepreneur who was in the B-pictures and was having an affair with Gloria Swanson. He didn't have enough family money to get into the B-pictures, but on a whim the former Jewish proprietor had offered him the hotel for a song. They'd worked out an arrangement and the old man had left L.A. for Palm Springs for convalescence after wrestling with cancer. A sharp-dressed little man with dark, tanned skin showed up each week to pick up the envelope; Mick wondered if he was carrying a gun beneath his silk outfit—his dark eyes staring with tremendous leverage. He pondered what would happen if that envelope were light one week, if the shylock would request Jimmy's flesh in return for his default.

● ● ●

"How's the new baby?" asked Jimmy with a smile.

"She's grand," said Mick nervously.

"And the wife?"

"Well, she's just grand, Jim."

He nodded and Mick looked at Gabriel, who was talking with some other men.

"Listen, I've got something for you," he began, nodding to a pint glass.

Mick nodded and poured him a Guinness, and quickly set it on the bar.

"What's on your mind?" asked Mick, his heart skipping a beat.

"I've made an investment. I've put money into a movie." He sipped his stout.

"Really," replied Mick.

"Yeah, a Western. It's something that Joe is involved in. He asked me to come on board and I couldn't resist. I mean, that's why we really came out here, right? Hollywood. If I wanted to run a shebeen, I could've just as well done that back home."

Mick looked at him incredulously. This seemed like the opportunity he had been waiting for. He smiled. "Well, that's grand. What can I do to help?"

"I want you to be my man on the set, make sure things run smoothly, if you know what I mean."

"Out where, exactly?"

"Santa Clarita, about forty miles east."

Mick nodded and felt the twinge in his stomach again. He imagined living in the desert, far away from this seaside city he had become so attached to. What would Shannon say? But this was his opportunity to move up in the McLean gang.

"I have a feeling that this Jazz Age stuff is fading," said Jimmy. "People are getting into country music—more like our sound, you know? When I was back in Chicago, I heard this guy, Gene Autry, on the radio. It's a good sound."

Mick looked at his boss as he spoke in a most-obsessed manner. What would Shannon say? He kept thinking. She was a bit of a pessimist, especially if the money wasn't flowing in as he'd promised. He wondered what the catch was.

"Of course," continued Jimmy. "There'd also be a house there for you."

Mick's eyes lit up. A house? The idea of owning a home was one that had evacuated his mind as soon as they arrived in California. It would be at least a year, maybe more, before they had enough for anything.

"I'll have to run it by the wife," said Mick. "See how she feels."

Jimmy smiled and finished his stout. He wiped his mouth, stood, and stared disdainfully at Gabriel, who was walking toward them. Jimmy looked deep into Mick's green eyes, reached out, and took his face into his hands, pulling it close.

"Sometimes," he whispered, "you have to be a man. You have to decide when there's a good opportunity put forth for your family. Back in Boston, you'd be a slave in the union for life apprenticing with your Da at some waterworks. I'm only offering once."

He gave him a kiss on the cheek then turned to the crowd and shouted, *Lá Fhéile Pádraig!* "Happy St. Patrick's Day!" The crowd responded by cheering rambunctiously. The pianist struck up "Sweet Adeline" and the men sang a few verses before Jimmy quieted them down. He took Gabriel by the neck and turned him toward Mick, who came around the other side of the bar. Jimmy threw his arm around him as well. It was as if they were back in Dorchester, making teams for stickball.

"Lads—let me introduce the newest candidate for city selectmen—Gabriel Bradley!" he exclaimed.

Gabriel smiled at Mick, who was trying to let it all sink in. It was too late; he was part of it now. In the dark shebeen, the music began again. And Mick already knew what he would tell Shannon.

*

On Sunday afternoon, after Mass, Gabriel packed the new Ford with a picnic basket, blankets, folding chairs, and towels. He had slicked his hair back, parted it in the middle, and slid his dark sunglasses on. His outfit was that of a tourist: Bermuda shorts and a collared short-sleeve shirt with sandals. This was the day he would tell Shannon about the plan, about how he'd been chosen. It could be worse: Jimmy could be using him for muscle or asking him to take care of collecting from the gamblers who played cards in the shebeen on Saturday nights. These were the men who sometimes ended up in the Los Angeles aqueduct floating face down with their throats slashed. He called out to Shannon, who was getting the kids together, saying that he was ready as he tried to shake the image from his mind.

Mick steered the Ford steadily down Ocean Boulevard as they headed south toward Manhattan Beach. One of the other barmen had a driveway at his flat near the beach where they could park. It was a beautiful day and Mick glanced at his wife holding Sinéad, the infant, on her lap, while Liam sat in the back staring out at the surfers riding waves. He would wait until they were on the beach to tell her. It was hard to get angry on the beach; it was a place of solace, especially for a fair Dorchester girl who only knew Revere and Nantasket.

They arrived and got settled on the shore, close to the water. The baby played with a sand pail and Liam ran back and forth between their umbrella and chairs and the water. Mick watched his son and wondered if his pale skin would burn underneath the midday sun.

He studied his son's physique; he was going to be an athletic kid, and the idea of moving away from Santa Monica disappointed him. What kind of schools would they have in Santa Clarita? Mick had hoped to send him to the Catholic school with the nuns situated behind St. Monica's.

He had heard that Will Rogers was shooting movies out there and that was about it—there were farms and agricultural workers—something that was changing in Los Angeles. Goldwyn Pictures had filmed most of their silent flickers between there and Hollywood. Gene Autry, the singer Jimmy had mentioned, was also coming out from Chicago, according to an article he had read in the *Times*. It was an exciting time.

Shannon looked at him and smiled. He tried to smile back, but she knew him too well.

* * *

"What's on your mind, Darling?" she asked. "You look troubled."

"Is it that obvious?" he said.

"You wear concern on you face like a little boy," she continued, her lips curling up in the same way they had years ago when he had timidly asked if he could kiss her goodnight. It had been at the end of their first date to an ice cream parlor in Dorchester.

It suddenly occurred to Mick that his wife had started to lose her Irish accent in the three years they'd been in California.

"So, what do you want me to tell you?" he asked.

"Tell me that you have some good news," she said.

"I think I do, but I'm not sure. I mean, I don't know what you'll—Well, you see—"

"Mick—I'm pregnant," Shannon interrupted.

He looked at her, shocked, then stood and stared out at the Pacific.

"Pregnant?" he repeated. All he could think of was home—Boston—moving the family back away from all this—abandoning paradise.

"Aren't you happy?" Shannon finally asked.

Mick looked down at his wife. Her face was overwhelmed with disappointment and her bottom lip began to curl. He immediately dropped his knees to the sand, wrapped his arms around her, and kissed the top of her head, then her lips—long.

"Yes, yes," he reassured her. "We'll name him Patrick, after Gabriel's brother. If a girl, Patricia."

"Are you sure?"

He kissed her forehead. "Yes, of course. It's wonderful."

"I'm glad. So, what were you going to tell me?"

Mick held his balance then looked at her and smiled weakly. He reached for his cigarettes and put one between his lips. "Nothing," he said. "I just wanted to ask you if you wanted to look at that little bungalow you had your eye on off San Vicente?"

"Can we afford it?"

* * *

"Not today," he said, blowing smoke into the warm air as he waved out the match flame. "But maybe someday soon."

Shannon smiled, leaned over, and kissed him on the cheek. She rose and ran toward Liam, who was floating dangerously deeper in the ocean, pulled by the undertow. Mick threw his cigarette in the sand and picked up his daughter who smiled at him, then looked out and pointed.

"*Wa-wah, Dadda!*" she said.

He would tell Shannon later, maybe after her second Martini. He would tell her that there was no other option.

*

Mick stood at the bar. It was Holy Thursday and the crowd would be arriving after Mass for a few drinks before the Catholic sacrifices of Good Friday. He turned and stared into the Jameson mirror behind the bar, studying the wrinkling forehead which forty days ago was adorned with blackened ashes in the form of a cross. So much had happened since then—most notably, that Gabriel had won the early April election.

He'd put Shannon and the kids on a train to Santa Clarita the day before at Union Station. Jimmy had made all the arrangements and the house would be waiting for them. Mick was to join them in two days if everything went as planned.

Gabriel walked in and called out to Mick. He approached the bar and Mick began to pour him a stout.

"None for me, I'm a councilman, now," Gabriel laughed. "Don't want that in the papers. Government official drinking during Prohibition."

Mick stopped the tap and pushed back up. He dumped the stout down the drain.

"You're a changed man already, Mr. Bradley," joked Mick.

Gabriel looked at Mick seriously and leaned forward on the bar.

"Mick—we need to talk."

* * *

Mick nodded and looked around to see if they had privacy.

"It's Jimmy," began Gabriel. "He's been a little aggressive lately. It's awkward."

He looked at his old friend. There was fear on Gabriel's face—real fear.

"Jimmy asked me to do something, you know, something illegal…" Then he stopped and stared at Mick.

Mick nodded. "Well, just don't do it."

"We can't talk about this here," Gabriel whispered. "We'll have to do it outside—later. Where shall we meet?"

The door opened and a crowd of men marched in from Mass at St. Monica's.

"We can meet at the pier, around midnight," said Mick.

"But it's got to be tonight," his friend insisted.

Mick watched as Gabriel put on his straw hat then moved through the crowd of men coming for their final drinks before the abstemiousness of Good Friday. He stepped back and looked down again at the revolver, then thought of Shannon, Liam, and Sinéad out in Santa Clarita.

*

Mick finished his shift and took the last trolley west to the Santa Monica Pier, nervously considering what was about to happen. He walked the length of the pier past the Ferris wheel, thinking he was certain he had seen this same dock in a flicker he took Shannon to when he was courting her back in Dorchester. Her father had demanded she be home by eight o'clock sharp, and finally approved of Mick after he'd kept his agreement to the curfew five times. When they first arrived in Santa Monica, he and Shannon had seen a beach-beauty contest at the bottom of the pier on one of their Saturday walks, but Mick didn't think any of those girls were as pretty as his wife.

Mick reached the end of the pier and spotted Gabriel sitting on a bench, lighting a cigarette. He heard the crash of the Pacific rolling in from Santa Monica Bay beneath them as it snapped against the wooden support beams.

Gabriel nodded to him and Mick sat on the bench lighting a Camel and looking over at the tired face of his friend. He usually liked to stand at the end of the pier, elbows on the edge of the wood railing. But he was happy to sit after being on his feet all night at the shebeen.

"Heard from Shannon, yet?" Gabriel asked.

Mick reached into his jacket and took out a Western Union telegram.

"They're fine. Settling in. The house is a bit smaller than she'd hoped for, but it's a house. I'll be heading out in the morning on the eight o'clock train from Union Station."

Gabriel nodded and put out his cigarette.

"Jimmy has to go, Mick," said Gabriel.

Mick paused, but remained calm. "What has he gotten you into?" asked Mick.

"Oil. He wants me to lobby for a site in Beverly Hills. There's a well underneath a residential neighborhood. But there are children all around—and he still wants to dig. It'll require bribes of influential council members and possibly a little muscle—and all that leads back to me." He sighed. "I told him no, that I wouldn't use my influence. He told me that he has some things on me—bad things, Mick. Things that could get me tossed off this pier."

Mick nodded and lit another Camel. He wanted to walk—walk away from it all. He wanted to be with his family, hold his son on his lap, and not worry. He reached into his pocket and Gabriel watched nervously. He removed his wallet, fingered inside it, and handed him an old photograph—the only photograph he actually had. Gabriel studied it and laughed.

"Hell, this is from ten years ago," Gabriel beamed. "Your wedding day—look how thin we were."

Mick looked at the three of them—Jimmy, Gabriel, and he, posing with Shannon who was dressed in the ivory lace wedding gown that she now kept safely in a department store box in the closet. Gabriel handed him back the photograph and Mick slid it back inside his wallet.

"We pledged something that day," said Mick. "You were both in my wedding—you were my best man, Gabriel."

Gabriel nodded and leaned to the side.

* * *

Mick stood.

"I'll take care of everything," said Mick. "You won't have to worry about anything anymore."

Gabriel looked down.

"Can you do it tonight, Mick?"

"Yeah—tonight everything will be settled. All debts will be paid."

Silence.

They stood together and Mick hugged his childhood friend.

"Thank you," Gabriel whispered.

He began to walk away and Mick reached into his jacket again, muttered a prayer in Gaelic, then pulled the trigger twice. The force pushed Gabriel back against the wooden railing at the end of the pier. Mick squeezed out a third shot and watched his friend barrel into the gushing waves beneath the pier.

Mick quickly tossed the revolver over the railing. He was in shock, but did not wait to hear it collide with the water below. He ran back down the pier to the car that was promised to be waiting for him, with nothing but his family on his mind.

GABRIEL—THE PROTECTOR

The idea of killing the old man never appealed to me. It was Anton who came up with the devious plan to dispose of my employer of ten years. Anton was a thirty-something Serbian expatriated mercenary who had come out to Los Angeles to find fame and fortune after fighting in the Yugoslav Wars as a teenager. His nature was brutal. He had killed several men—according to him—in a number of different ways.

Anton spoke of using automatic weapons; slashing men's throats with knives; and even a tale where he stuffed a hand grenade down his enemy's pants, blowing him—all of him—to smithereens. He was quite familiar with death; growing up, it had been all around him.

However, the old man had been good to me. When I arrived in Los Angeles, I aspired to be a screenwriter. He was a retired movie director who had offered me a job as his personal assistant out of his palatial mansion, which was tucked neatly in Laurel Canyon just above Studio City. He had been a legend and I was a mere novice in a new city—looking to him for wisdom and sustenance. He had paid me a meager wage to start, but when his health began to fade I became more of a caretaker for him—handling his affairs, paying his bills and, at times, feeding and bathing him. He was appreciative of my kind nature and although his faculties were fading, I was sure he cared for me like a father cares for a son. I had no reason to wish him ill and he knew my character to be quite reputable. It seemed in a town where no one looks out for anyone but themselves, we needed each other to survive.

Anton, however, had struggled with his acting career and side-job as leg-breaker for a loan shark out of Hollywood. He saw the old man as an easy moneymaking opportunity. He would often visit me at the mansion and disappear into the old man's office, sifting through files and examining bank ledgers. His scavenger hunt produced two things that he desired—a million-dollar life insurance policy taken out in the 1950s, and a healthy bank account.

"He's near death, anyway, Gabriel," he'd often say to me. "What's the difference if he dies in his sleep or if a pillow is pressed over his face?"

I stared at Anton, horrified by his intention.

"You're a psycho," I said to him. "And besides, this man is a legend. Don't you think that the police would be a little suspicious if money disappeared from his accounts?"

"No," he replied frankly. "He's a hundred years old, far from the spotlight—no one would suspect a thing. No one remembers him."

Then, Anton would go to the bathhouse, change into his bathing suit, and go for an afternoon swim in the old man's pool beneath the warm summer sun. I shook my head and went to empty the old man's bedpan.

The old man had directed many Hollywood stars: Cary Grant, Burt Lancaster, Montgomery Clift, and even Marilyn Monroe. He had won some Oscars and even a lifetime achievement award from the Directors Guild, but much to my chagrin Anton was correct: he was forgotten. He'd gotten divorced in the sixties when he faded from the limelight, and his wife had moved to New York and died in the eighties. There were no children, no close relatives. The studios had broken contact with him and just about everyone from his generation was dead. No one came by the house to check on him. No one cared, besides me and my militant Serbian friend who wanted to steal his fortune.

* * *

I came upon the old man in his bed one afternoon and studied his emaciated form underneath the bedcovers. He was a skeleton, suffering from the effects of cancer and emphysema. The idea of his demise had made me quit smoking because of the daily pain I witnessed him in. He had an arsenal of medication lined up on his bedside table and I played doctor, giving him his dosage and refilling prescriptions on a monthly basis. I removed his soiled bedpan and quietly disposed of it in the bathroom.

Anton appeared back at the door, half-naked with a towel around his waist and water dripping from his body. He reminded me of a brute, someone Tennessee Williams might have cast as Stanley Kowalski in *A Streetcar Named Desire*. He was a man capable of tremendous leverage and I was a failed writer-turned-weak-caretaker.

"Look at the poor soul; he's as good as dead. Really look at him, Gabriel. He's suffering," said Anton.

He moved toward the bed, as I flushed the toilet, and snapped his fingers at the old man.

"He's in a coma. He'd never feel a thing. It would be like euthanasia," he said harshly. "Let me get my gun in the car. I'd be doing him a favor."

I waved him away angrily.

"Do not disrespect him," I scolded. "He can hear you."

Anton nodded his head, resigned to my loyalty and respect for the old man. He exited the room, making his way down the marble staircase as I finished my duties.

I had written several screenplays, which the old man had critiqued for me from his wheelchair. He even tried to push one to one of his old studios, but his contacts were gone—he had no connection to Hollywood anymore. He taught me well, helping me to structure my acts, shape my dialogue and characters, and instructing me on storytelling in his old age. He would sit in his favorite recliner and stare down into Laurel Canyon as I read him a scene or two. He'd encourage me to read Chekhov's plays, Freud's psychology, Tolstoy's short stories, whatever I could get my hands on. He was a learned man, a scholar who had graduated from Harvard before heading West to make his fortune. He'd started where I was—an assistant, then a staff writer at Paramount, then slowly he

* * *

became a director in the days of big studios. He'd spent time with James Dean and it was rumored that he'd planned to write the movie of his career when the unfortunate car crash happened. It still hurt him to talk about it.

"Such fire inside," he'd say. "He was troubled, but his passion was like an inferno."

We'd dine together each night and I'd prepare his favorite meals like prime rib and mashed potatoes while he still had his appetite. We'd sit on his back terrace by a flaming fire pit and discuss life, family, and commitment. He had tremendous values, old-school values, and it seemed that he'd rather attend a USC football game at The Coliseum or watch Koufax pitch at Dodger Stadium than direct films.

But the cancer came fast. Or perhaps it sat dormant inside him for years. He would cough and cough until finally, blood appeared. I took him to his doctor, an old Jewish physician down in Beverly Hills on the other side of the canyon, but the doctor told me that, frankly, there was nothing that could be done. He suggested experimental studies and drugs as well as alternative medicine, but the old man refused.

"I'm not going to be some guinea pig for experimental medicine," he'd stammered.

I drove him back over the hill to his safe citadel, and he remained silent the whole way. It was if he was paralyzed by the thought of death.

About two weeks later, Anton called me on my cell phone and told me to meet him at DuPar's on Ventura for breakfast. The old man was napping, so I took the keys to his Bentley and made my way down the windy canyon through the tight traffic to the restaurant. Anton had secured a booth and sat sipping a coffee.

"Gabriel, my friend. How are you?" he asked, rising to shake my hand as if this was a business meeting. I nodded at him and signaled to the Hispanic waitress that I wanted a coffee.

"So, what do you want this time, Anton? Planning another murder?" I asked.
He laughed and nodded.

"I deserve that—I know," he said. "I didn't mean to insult you or the old man. It's just that you get to live a life of luxury in the hills, and I am down here struggling to make ends meet. I thought you'd want to share it with me."

"Anton," I said. "It's my job, and it's not a pretty one. The things I have to do—I'm like a nurse."

He laughed at the idea.

"A nurse? You have a mansion, a car, and money. You are living like a king. So what if you have to give the old man a couple of shots or clean his bedpan."

I shook my head and the waitress arrived to take our order. I opted for eggs Benedict and Anton went with a Belgian waffle with strawberries and whipped cream.

"Okay, here's my idea," he said.

"Here we go," I replied.

"No, I want you to hear me out. I've been doing some research. There is a storm coming, massive rains. There will be flooding in the canyon and extreme dampness, do you understand?"

"No."

"If the old man gets a cold, perhaps from being in a damp place for a while, like his wine cellar, he will catch a cold and die naturally."

"We're not doing this, Anton," I whispered. "Are you mad?"

"A little. But I have something that will change your mind very quickly, Gabriel."

Anton reached into his leather sack and lifted out a document. At the top, it read: *Last Will and Testament.*

"What is that?" I asked.

He raised his eyebrows and smiled.

"The other day, I found this in his desk. It was revised about two years ago. Take a look at the beneficiary of his estate."

I took the papers from Anton and scanned them quickly. It became very clear that the old man had left everything to me.

"The mansion, the car, the money, it's all yours, Gabriel," he said. "That is—when he dies."

I set the papers down and looked at Anton. I figured I'd be in the will somehow when the old man died, but this was truly unexpected. I'd gone from an hourly paid assistant to a millionaire. The idea made me tingle.

The waitress brought our breakfast and we ate in silence. By the time we were finished, I had made up my mind.

"Okay, meet me at the mansion tonight," I said. "When the rains come, we'll settle this once and for all."

Anton smiled and took the check.

"I'm proud of you, Gabriel," he said. "Allow me to treat you to breakfast."

*

The old man's wine cellar was worth a million on its own. He had vintages from all over California, as well as France, Spain, and Italy. It was sunk beneath the mansion, its bricks shifting with each earthquake over the years. But it was damp, very damp. Just a few minutes down there made me sneeze and develop congestion. Anton was right—a whole night down there could kill someone.

The rains came as darkness fell, and I bathed the old man and gave him his pills as lightning flashed over the canyon. I put him in his best pajamas and he smiled, trying to thank me, but his words were slurred from his dementia.

Around midnight, Anton rang the doorbell and I made my way down the stairs to greet him. I told him that the old man was waiting upstairs and that the plan was in place. He smiled and slapped my back.

"We're going to be rich," he said joyously.

"You'll never have to work another day of your life," I replied with a smile.

I insisted that we make sure the wine cellar was ready for our work, and we descended the steps as Anton surveyed the situation.

"You can fit a whole body here," he said, indicating a compartment in the floor. "This place is spooky. Like a morgue."

I selected a bottle of Italian wine and smiled at Anton.

"You sure you want to do this—kill the innocent old man?" I asked him frankly.

"Never felt so sure about anything in my life," he said.

"Good," I replied, taking the bottle of wine by the neck.

Anton knelt down for a moment, as if he was going to say a prayer. He was studying the compartment in the floor. I raised the bottle of wine high in the air. As it came down on his head, the red Chianti mixed with his blood and he fell forward into the compartment, just big enough to fit his frame.

I spent a few hours doing my masonry work, creating a level floor in the wine cellar with some leftover bricks from the original construction of the mansion. When I was done, I washed up, walked up the spiral staircase to the old man's room, and sat with him late into the night watching the rains fall from the sky.

* * *

LAYOVER

The night my mother died, I was on Sunset Boulevard—drunk. I was also drunk on Olympic—but that was much later in the evening when I arrived back in Santa Monica. After dinner on the Strip, I took a limo down Wilshire with my agent from CAA, Max Sackostein, back to The Buffalo Club. I was smoking cigarettes on the patio while we were celebrating the bidding war on my screenplay, *Tracks*. However, unbeknownst to me, my mother was suffering her final moments on the bathroom floor of my childhood home back in Massachusetts.

My mother dying couldn't have occurred at a more inconvenient time: I had finally made it. After spending the previous six years living on Chef Boyardee and cheap cigarettes, trying to figure out how to scale the mighty walls of Rome with 120 pages of paper, I'd realized success. It had been a meandering path between writing boot camps in Burbank, two-day film schools in Sherman Oaks, internships in Studio City, and then a necessary teaching job, which I hated, at my wife's demand. It was a path that had me rubbing elbows with my students' famous parents at cocktail parties and barbecues in the Palisades.

As I smoked my fifth victory cigarette on the back patio of The Buffalo Club, I imagined myself like Julius and Philip Epstein after they finished adapting Rick's Place into *Casablanca*. They must've felt like this—euphoric. They must've known.

I remember mailing copies of that screenplay off from the Santa Monica post office in manila envelopes to some of those parent-agents I had schmoozed with at the barbecues in the Palisades. Three days later, I arose to the sound of my cell phone vibrating on my dresser, and when I saw CAA on the caller ID, I knew my life was about to change.

I now had the fat Jewish agent—check; I had the beautiful Californian wife—check; I had money in the bank—check. But after that night at The Buffalo Club, I felt like I had nothing.

I missed the first call that night from my father on my cell—the one in which he desperately informed me that my sixty-year-old mother had collapsed on the bathroom floor and was having trouble breathing. In retrospect, at that point in the evening, I recall having had an Amstel in my left hand, a Camel in my right, and talking to Max about a movie deal. I remember him backing away from me politely because he didn't like the smoke in his face. But that's the thing—he didn't walk away, either; this was a business discussion. He was telling me that Luke Wilson's manager liked the script and was strongly recommending it to his client. It seems a lot can happen to your world overnight.

I did answer the second call. I heard my father crying. Panicked, I excused myself from Max and immediately moved out of the crowded, noisy courtyard. With my other hand still holding the cigarette and blocking my ear, I struggled to understand my father's diatribe. I made it through the main bar and out onto Olympic, where a line of scantily dressed women waited to get in. I remember it being warm for an October night, although a cool zephyr blew back my long hair and brushed against my tan skin.

"Dad—slow down. I can't understand you," I said. The bouncer—a former linebacker at USC— nodded to me in concern.

"You okay?" he asked. I waved him off, moved out into the street, and then to the grass strip away from the crowd.

"What happened, Dad? I can't understand you," I yelled into my cell, as if yelling was going to control my father's hysteria some 3,000 miles away.

"Your mother just went in the ambulance," he finally got out. "They took her to Mass General. Her stomach hurt all day."

"Okay, okay. Hold on. Let me think," I said.

"I have to go," he said. "There's blood. I have to clean up."

"Blood?"

"Call your sister."

"Of course, Dad. Right away."

"I have to go. I love you."

Click.

I felt my body twitch. A wave of dizziness came over me, and I reached out and held onto a blue sign that read, "Welcome to Beautiful Santa Monica" in green-and-red lettering.

I then realized it was the first time my father had said he loved me since the day I left for college twelve years before. Although he had yelled at me constantly throughout my youth, I desperately wanted to hear his voice. I wanted him to give me a speech about responsibility, tell me I needed to get my priorities in order. I yearned for him to tell me that if I hadn't been so goddamned selfish to move out to California, I'd be standing at my fallen mother's bedside.

I heard the ocean rumbling a mile away, I heard a seagull cry out, I heard the drone of the 405 Freeway, I heard the music and laughter from The Buffalo Club. It was happening, really happening— my mother was dying. I'd known it would happen someday, but I guess I didn't figure it would be in the middle of a drunken Saturday night in the middle of Santa Monica. She had looked older the last time I saw her at my uncle's funeral. I remember thinking it was only a matter of time. I threw down my cigarette. She'd smoked them since I was child and it had been the source of constant criticism from my old man, which had annoyed me as a child. I wondered if she'd smoked because he wouldn't let up on her. I wondered why I'd taken on the habit myself. Genetics, probably.

I looked over at The Buffalo Club, wondering what to do next. Max came jogging across Olympic with a concerned look on his face. He had on a blue sport coat and caches. He straightened his black

Armani glasses, caught his breath, and stared at me critically.

"What gives?" he asked.

"My mother's dying," I said, without expression, as I studied the crowd outside the club. For some reason, at that exact moment, I found it intriguing that the majority of the women waiting were blonde and had larger-than-normal breasts, and that many of the patrons inside were short, dark-haired, unattractive men. Max's eyes opened wide and he covered his mouth, then came closer and gently put his hand on my back to comfort me.

"Oh—shit," he said softly. "I'm fucking—sorry. Let me think." He seemed to be sure that a phone call to somebody in Beverly Hills would magically change my mother's health condition back in Boston.

I turned away and dialed my sister's number in Brookline, but got her voicemail. Then I tried my wife but got her voicemail, too, as she was out with friends in Westwood.

Nobody was home.

Max had picked up his cell and was talking to someone. I nodded to him.

"I have to fly back," I said, walking away.

Max nodded and I heard his phone ring again.

"Let me give you a ride," he shouted. "What about the jet? I can get you the private jet. Let me call Harv."

"Take the call, Max," I shouted, not turning around as I made my way across Olympic.

"Just don't sell the damn script until I come back. I want to be there to meet Luke Wilson."

And with that, I left my fat Jewish agent alone on the median strip of Olympic. I looked back at The Buffalo Club, heard the patrons laughing on the patio. None of it mattered.

I started walking home.

Santa Monica is a strange place. Part beach community, part industrial, part luxury neighborhood, part city. I first lived on 11th Street, a mere mile from The Buffalo Club, but the neighborhoods change as you head toward the ocean, or in my case, Montana Avenue. Olympic is a boulevard, where they routed the 1984 Olympic Marathon as it departed Santa Monica College. I remember watching it on television when I was a kid and thinking that it would be cool to live in California someday, even though it hovered around 100 degrees at race time. Olympic is the industrialized part of town: buildings that used to be factories, now production studios and art galleries. Further down is Crossroads School where misdirected, artsy, and filthy-rich kids go when they can't get into Loyola, Harvard-Westlake, or Marymount—or just want to focus on something less academic. My friend, Schwartzman, said he had a cousin who had gone to Crossroads and that he had seen Kate Hudson at that cousin's bat mitzvah when he was a kid.

I made my way up 11th, past the Salvation Army store where my wife and I bought our first furniture. I thought about the old desk and beat-up leather chair that I'd donated back to the place when I got my first residual for an episode of *Stand Up Teacher*, a one-man play turned sitcom.

I passed over Wilshire by El Cholo and J.P.s, past the old apartment we used to rent where I wrote *Tracks*, then eventually over Montana. The avenue, which is usually bustling with shoppers, people biking to the beach, joggers, yoga class attendees, was dead quiet. A traffic light held red and swayed gently in the breeze coming off the sea. I stopped for a moment and strained and heard the ocean just a mile away. To the north, I heard a coyote howling in the canyon.

It was a Saturday night in Santa Monica, and my mother was dying back in Boston.

My place was on Marguerita—just above Montana Avenue. I sold it the previous year as part of the settlement. Marguerita runs all the way to Ocean where you can look out at the Pacific from the Bluffs. Its location is impeccable. I could walk twelve blocks to the beach, take yoga and spinning classes, or just sit in front of Pete's or Starbucks and compose my screenplays. I was in a great neighborhood with sitcom and movie stars.

I opened the front door and found that no one was home. The living room was as quiet as a morgue, and I checked my home phone for any more messages from my father. Nothing. I went upstairs and grabbed my suitcase out of the closet, threw it open on the dresser, then went to my walk-in closet. I saw my dark Brooks Brothers suit with three buttons hanging and grabbed it, as well as my

* * *
79

leather garment bag, and tossed it onto my silk-sheeted bed.

I grabbed my shaving kit, finished packing, went downstairs to the living room, and then set my luggage by the door and called for a car from a service that Max had recommended for the Golden Globes last year. I could make it to LAX in fifteen minutes down Lincoln tonight—open road straight through Venice and Playa Del Rey into Westchester. I called my wife again, but I got voicemail and angrily threw my phone toward the beige Pottery Barn couch. It clipped the coffee table and slammed against the hardwood floor. I lit a cigarette, even though my wife refused to let me smoke in the house, even though I paid for it, and headed to the medicine cabinet for an Ativan. I knew it was going to be a long journey home.

I learned later that as I had my selfish tirade in my living room, my mother was wheeled into Mass General on a stretcher bound for surgery on her rupturing aortic aneurysm. There had been a weak spot in her main line, probably due to something she was born with, a congenital defect, or perhaps one caused by a flaw or blow to the artery some time during her life. When the surgeon, an Italian man from the Medford, who had studied medicine at Harvard, opened her up, he knew that things were bad. The surgical procedure carries a ninety-percent failure rate—and this time was no different.

As the limo drove me through the darkness of Lincoln, past the prostitutes working the corner by the 7-Eleven, I imagined my father as he sat alone in the hospital waiting room watching the Red Sox-Yankees game in front of a coffee table with old, tattered copies of *Sports Illustrated* and *Better Housekeeping*. I imagined my sister had shown up later with her husband and five kids in pajamas. No one probably cried; they were in shock—or didn't comprehend the enormity of the situation. I envisioned them as they sat around and waited and waited until it was late and all the toys and coloring books had been gone through. Finally, I speculated that my brother-in-law took the kids home. The Italian doctor probably finally came down around midnight with a grim look on his face. I learned later that he told my father and sister that Mom made it through the surgery but there were tests to be run on brain activity. My sister and father ate a silent meal in the hospital cafeteria. After a few minutes, I imagined my sister getting up to call me, which she actually did. I was sitting in the Admiral's Club at

• • •

LAX on my third Jameson. I answered my banged-up, but still-functioning cell phone.

"Are you coming home?" she asked me.

"Yeah," I replied. "I'm at LAX. I just got a ticket—first class on American. I'll be there by nine tomorrow morning. I have a layover in Dallas for half an hour."

"A layover? Jesus—just hurry up," she said. "Get here."

"I'm in California. This isn't *Star Trek*."

"I think she's going to die. It's not good. She's cold."

"Cold?"

"The doctor said they're having trouble keeping her blood pressure up or something. We're going up to see her in a few minutes. Oh, God—I think I need to call a priest."

"Don't say that," I said, finishing my drink and shaking it at the Mexican bartender for another. "Don't say that, okay?"

Silence.

"Just come home," my sister replied sharply, and then hung up.

The bartender set the fourth Jameson in front of me and I downed it quickly. It burnt my throat and chest, but I wanted more and I wondered where my wife was.

I'd been flying the Logan International-to-LAX route since I was nineteen. My roommate back in Boston at Emerson was from Pacific Palisades and he would invite me out for breaks and vacations to stay at his family's house. California seemed so fun, then. We spent time at his beach club, hiked in the Will Rogers Park, did all the touristy things. I got to know the lie of the land as I rode a mountain bike all over the West Side—all the way to Manhattan Beach. But for two hundred bucks and up to a three-hour layover in Pittsburgh or Dallas, L.A. was my drug of choice.

As we rose up over Los Angeles, I thought back on how this all started. I guess it began when I came home one afternoon when I was twenty-five and opened a bottle of Sam Adams, then crashed on my couch in Brighton, Massachusetts. I was sick of teaching high school English and coaching

* * *

track—I felt there had to be something else. That afternoon the apartment seemed particularly cold, and I wondered if we were out of oil again, if we'd have to prime the valve. I was living with my roommates from college. We all had jobs and rented this shit-hole of a place off Market Street, two miles from Harvard Square. There were two Irish bars within half a mile. Someone had left the movie, *Rushmore*, on the dining room table. I popped it in and watched. Luke Wilson had a minor role—a doctor who was dating an English schoolteacher—and he was funny. The thing about Luke Wilson is that he's Luke Wilson, not Keanu Reeves. He could star in *Old School*, but he'd never be a star in *The Matrix*. He's a lover-boy actor—a marketable actor. So, after the movie was over and three more Sams were gone, I went out and bought Final Draft, a screenwriting program, and started typing.

For some reason, Luke Wilson reminded me of the cowboys in the Western movies I liked so much as a kid; I thought I might be able to recreate them.

When I arrived in Dallas, it was about three in the morning. I woke up from a short nap and followed everyone off the plane to the terminal. I studied the people in front of me—a line of zombies on the road to nowhere—with attaché cases, laptops, and sport coats over their arms. Dallas seemed like purgatory.

I needed to get to the terminal on the opposite side of the airport and felt my legs aching from the drinking I'd done earlier. The Dallas-Ft. Worth Airport has a monorail system, white trains that look like they belong in Disney World. I boarded one and noticed it was just me and a guy in a cowboy hat and jeans. The doors shut after a little alarm went off and we started moving. The dude looked at me but said nothing. We slowed down at the terminal, an alarm rang, and I got off. My priority, since I had a layover, was to have a cigarette before I got on the final four-hour flight. I found an exit to Terminal D and stood outside, smoking. It suddenly occurred to me that this was the same city Kennedy had landed in the day he was assassinated.

The sidewalk by the parking garage was empty, so after a couple of puffs I screamed. It was a loud barbaric yawp, a lamentation out to deal with the fact that I was 2,500 miles from my mother's deathbed. I lit another cigarette, then another, and finally just started laughing.

* * *

My cell phone rang and I picked it up quickly. It was my sister.

"Where the hell are you, now?" she said frantically.

"Dallas," I said.

"Well—she's in intensive care. But the doctors are optimistic."

"Optimistic? That doesn't sound good. Sounds like they are stalling to tell us the truth."

"Well, it's Dad who is worrying me right now. He doesn't understand what they're telling him. I can't explain the fact that his wife is dying."

I looked around and noticed that the cowboy was standing with one boot up on his duffle bag, tapping on the back of a pack of Marlboro Reds. I suddenly remembered my sister was pregnant again.

"Okay, okay. I'll be there in four hours," I said, looking at my watch. "Shit. I gotta go catch my flight."

I hung up and stared over at the cowboy. He looked like a character from my screenplay—a Western. I had written it more as an imitation of the cowboy movies I would watch with my mother when I was little. If late-night TV was showing a movie she wanted to see—a Western—I got to stay up late. That's how I grew up.

The cowboy tipped his hat again, and I moved through the sliding doors back into the airport, trying to forget his image.

As I sprinted toward my gate, I noticed something odd. The door behind the check-in desk was closed. Out of breath, I looked at the tired airline worker.

"What's going on?"

She looked up at me, and then over her shoulder. "The aircraft door is locked, Sir. You're going to have to rebook. 9-11 regulation. Nothing I can do. I'm sorry."

The next flight wasn't until ten in the morning. I never saw that cowboy again.

I called my wife on the way to the actual city of Dallas in a cab driven by a man who had an affection for modern country music. I figured I had some time to kill, so why not spend it away from the airport. She picked up.

* * *

"Where the hell are you?" she said in a tired and boozy voice.

"I'm in Dealey Plaza. By the Texas School Depository."

"What—?"

"Didn't you get my messages?"

"I lost my phone. I think I dropped it at a restaurant in Beverly Hills."

"I thought you were in Westwood."

"Yeah—that's what I meant. Where are you?"

"I told you. I'm in Dallas."

"Stop fooling around," she said.

"I'm on my way home. My mother—"

I felt myself getting emotional and put the phone to my chest for a minute. I knocked on the plastic sliding window. The cabbie looked back.

"Stop here, Pal," I said, handing him a Benjamin.

I got out and put my phone back to my ear, looking around Dealey Plaza. I imagined Lee Harvey Oswald aiming his rifle out the window.

"What's wrong with your mother?" my wife asked. It was the calmest I had heard her in months.

"I don't really know. She collapsed. An aneurysm."

I looked out to the roadway and imagined Kennedy's skull exploding. Jackie crawling up the back of the limo.

"I'm getting up right now—I'll fly out to meet you as soon…"

"Stay," I said in a firm voice.

"What? Why?"

"I'll call you when I know what's going on."

"I love you," she said. I couldn't remember the last time she had told me that.

"I'm going." And I hung up.

I met my wife in a Hollywood bar. She was looking for an agent who drove a BMW and who had

• • •

stood her up for drinks. Instead, she got a screenwriter who drove a Subaru. I made it very clear that writing was a priority for me, and was the sole reason that I'd moved 3,000 miles away from my family. Nothing—I told her—was going to get in my way.

We got married a year later in Santa Barbara in a small chapel near the beach by a Jesuit priest who was visiting from Ireland. It rained most of the time, but we rented a room at a bed-and-breakfast and drank champagne, spending our week away wandering the beach, bookstores, coffee shops, restaurants, and vineyards. When we got back to L.A., we started looking for houses with the $500,000 check I had made for script-doctoring work on a Universal project. My wife seemed to love me more as the money came in. And it was coming in after her wondering if I would ever sell anything.

However, over the last year, I had seen her wander away from me, and I had just let her go. I consciously decided to not fix the marriage. Instead, I pretended that everything was fine. My mother would often say to me as a child, "Say a prayer; everything will be fine." But as I sat on the tarmac at Dallas, I knew that everything was not fine.

After I had signed my deal with CAA, I found myself feeling quite empty. One Sunday, I walked around the corner to St. Monica's. Part of me wanted to ask God for strength to fix my marriage. The homily that day was given by a Mexican priest, who was visiting from a village near Cabo San Lucas on the Baja Peninsula. A pandemic had broken out and over a hundred children had died. Their Catholic parents came to him, angrily asking why God had let their children die and why He had not answered their prayers. The priest had smiled and said, "When we pray we want an answer from God. In this case, He did answer you, but His answer was— no."

I flew from Dallas to Pittsburgh the next morning. On the way, I started thinking back on my time with Mom. It was the two of us in the beginning, before my sister was born. Me, Mom, and cowboy movies late at night when she would let me stay up over my father's protest.

She was a teacher, but quit to have children. I think she missed her days with her students and correcting essays, but she spent her time teaching me. By the age of five, I had written my first short story—a rip-off of *David Copperfield*. By the time I was ten, she was sending my poetry and letters to the editor of the local paper. My mother took pride in my creativity. My father wanted me to play sports.

As I grew up and she grew older, sitting at the kitchen table, smoking her Salem 100s and obsessively doing crossword puzzles, I began to compose. It started with essays that I wrote on an old family Smith Corona that she edited with red pens, tearing apart my verb tense and dangling modifiers. By fifteen, I had a regular gig with the local newspaper as a sports reporter; by nineteen, I was writing for the *Sunday Globe*. When I was going through things after the funeral, I found a whole scrapbook my mother had kept with every article I had published along with some Mother's Day cards I'd written to her.

She'd kept it all. Including her marriage.

Suddenly the captain came on.

"Folks, we're experiencing a bit of turbulence. We're going to have to stop at a little airfield near Kansas City."

I looked at my watch and sighed; it was six minutes after six in the morning. I later learned that at the exact moment we were setting down on that runway in Missouri, my mother died. I read it later on her death certificate when I went to the hospital to pick up her wedding ring, her watch, and a gold shamrock necklace. They gave them to me in a plastic bag at a window located in the basement.

I had left at three in the morning on a Sunday, and somehow, between stops in Dallas, Kansas City, Pittsburgh, and Newark, I finally arrived home on Monday evening. I imagined that a priest had come and given her last rites. I imagined that they had wheeled her cold body down to the morgue and then my friend, who ran the funeral home, was called to come get the body and prepare it for the wake. I imagined that flowers were displayed around her casket, and a meeting with my father and sister was held to make all the arrangements.

I imagined my mother sitting in one of the folding chairs, smoking a Salem 100, and laughing at it all. She hated the pomp and circumstance of funerals, people showing up to pay their respects when they hadn't called or written in years; bunch of phonies. She hated when people made a fuss. It seemed so unnecessary to her.

* * *

I was just happy to be back. I wanted to sit with Dad and my sister and tell stories. I wanted to see the outpouring from the community who had come to celebrate her spirit. I took out my cell phone. It was dead. But I didn't want to talk to anyone anyway.

The cab dropped me off in front of the funeral home. I looked at my watch—it was too late— calling hours were over. I set down my suitcase, looked around, and then straightened the now-wrinkled Brooks Brothers suit that I had put on in the bathroom at Logan International. I was finally home.

Dad walked out of the funeral home, wiping his eyes and his bald head with his embroidered handkerchief. He was wearing his gray flannel suit. It was a hot October day, and I threw my cigarette down and then stomped on it quickly before he caught my eye. He finally turned and saw me and then shook his head, slowly walking toward me, his Wright shoe heels clicking against the sandy sidewalk.

"You're late," he said loudly. I had missed my own mother's wake. "Harry Goddamn Hollywood— what do you have to say for yourself?"

I smiled, leaned forward, and then hugged him. It felt good. I hope he thought the same. I was home again. Finally, he pushed me back and adjusted the shoulders of my three-button Brooks Brothers jacket.

"Nice three-button suit. But you need a haircut and a shave."

I wiped my eyes and laughed. "I know," I said.

"Want to go get some dinner?" he asked. "The game's coming on and I don't want to be around all these people."

I picked up my suitcase. "I'd like that," I said.

He nodded. "Me, too."

SAVING ARABS

I am standing in the playground behind the scarlet brick building that used to be my junior high, waiting for my five-year-old son to come down the slide. Instead, he retreats and I dash around, catching him just as he leaps off the ladder. He wiggles free from my grasp and sprints to a safer part of the playground. I breathe a sigh of relief, then turn and shake my head at my childhood friend, Mayo, who is sipping a hot Dunkin' Donuts coffee on this cool fall afternoon.

"Kid's got energy," he remarks.

"It's kind of a bonus feature," I reply.

"Hey, you know that painting with the towel-heads?" my childhood friend says, nodding toward our old school. "The one on the auditorium wall with the camel-jockeys holding guns?"

Now thirty-five, Mayo dons a salt-and-pepper mullet, goatee, and wears a leather jacket and jeans.

"Don't talk that way," I whisper. "He'll repeat it."

"Relax," says Mayo. "He doesn't know a Muslim from a Mormon."

* * *

I turn back to my son, who plays in the sandbox.

"Well, I'd like to protect him for a while," I say.

"Good luck. Your parents couldn't shelter you."

I look at him disdainfully. We grew up together and childhood friends say things that are brutally honest sometimes. Mayo and I share this ability because of our past.

"So, anyway," Mayo says, "that painting with the militant Arabs?"

"I remember it vaguely."

"Well, somebody appraised it at…" he pauses for effect, "one million bucks."

I whistle. Mayo always had the inside information, ever since he was a kid. He never left our hometown, opting to spend his days as a painter; an interior and exterior house painter, that is.

"I thought that thing was a fake," I say.

"Nope. And the town wants to sell it. Cash in." Mayo taps his pack of cigarettes and offers me one.

"No, thanks. I quit," I say.

"Jesus, five years in California…"

His laughter turns into a series of coughs. I shake my head and walk over to my son, who is now hanging from the monkey bars.

"It's happening soon," he says. "Some auction house in New York has it. Million bucks could help this town, considering what happened to the budget this year."

His words shouldn't bother me, but for some reason they are as vulgar as his bigoted language; a painting is being sold off by my town, and it suddenly makes me angry.

"You can speak at the next town meeting. Convince them to keep it," Mayo says confidently. "Like you did for the art program with that gay Jew senator who is now messing up the country with his mortgage reform program. Idiot."

I shake my head. "Frank Barney was a congressman, and that was different."

"Okay, okay. Sorry, that homo Hebrew congressman, my mistake," he whispers with a smirk. "Anyway, let's save this thing. You and me. We owe it to the town."

* * *

"Yeah, Mr. anti-Semite…I'm a little tied up lately." I nod to my son.

Mayo smiles and finishes his cigarette, putting it out in the sandbox. "Listen, you're still the same guy from when we were kids. You remember what we did? Right?"

I look at him, reluctant. "Kids do stupid stuff."

"But we still did it."

It's getting dark now. I call out to my son, who is wandering too close to the woods. New England is foreign to him, and seems a little strange to me at the moment; it's our first fall back from the West. I grab his hand as he protests.

"I have to get going," I call out to Mayo, who lights another cigarette in the wind. "I'll call you later."

"Your secret is safe with me, Old Buddy. Don't worry…I'll take it to the grave," his voice echoes.

I hold my son close and watch as Mayo walks toward his old beat-up Chevy, the same one he bought our senior year of high school. He sits inside, the embers of his cigarette burning. I open the door of my used Volvo for my son and he jumps in. But all I can think about is the painting with the Arabs in it.

*

When I was in junior high school, I let my mind wander during assemblies. I found myself daydreaming of Van Halen tapes, Air Jordans, Atari, and Ralph Lauren Polo shirts. I dreamt about a California mansion in Malibu, one with a swimming pool and a view of the ocean. I saw myself wandering the Sunset Strip with movie stars. I imagined my hometown tuning into MTV and seeing my tan image, commenting, "My, what a star he's made of himself!" It was during one of these assemblies that I first noticed the painting.

It hung on the wall of the auditorium. I recall thinking that it was massive and ugly. It depicted dark-skinned men adorned in turbans, sitting around in the middle of the desert. I remember wondering what they were waiting for. In the center of the painting sat an older, gray-haired man giving what appeared to be advice. They stood listening, holding rifles, with magazines of bullets draped about their shoulders. I imagined his words were philosophical; something about how life is abstract and they should give thanks and praise Allah.

Everything in the painting looked blurry. The colors were faded. One man's blue turban matched the sky above and, in an eccentric way, reminded me of the Virgin Mary. I remember staring at it and thinking that it must've been a fake. Later, I read that the painting, called *Arabs*, was a Spanish masterpiece by Juan Pablo Quixote-Santiago, a noted early twentieth-century artist. The Hawthornes, a rich family in town, had donated *Arabs* to our school for the town to enjoy back in the 1950s. But I just gawked at it, thinking it worthless and boring. I sought the MTV lifestyle.

My only real obsession in junior high was with drawing in my notebook during math class. I drew airplanes like the Concorde and the Harrier jet and obsessively sketched the Van Halen symbol. However, I didn't think what I was doing was artistic; it just killed time. During my eighth-grade year, I was forced to take a required art course and, after my teacher took notice, I was transferred into an advanced class that met in the basement of school during lunchtime study hall.

My parents seemed proud of me and my dad commented at dinner one night, "You always liked to draw, ever since you were a little guy. Well done, Son." And that was all I needed: I'd won my father's praise, which hadn't happened much in junior high. I began to draw obsessively, in hope that he might take notice again.

My work paid off. A large sketch of mine, depicting an F-16 in flight, was voted "Artwork of the Week" and featured in the display case near the main office. Even our principal, Mr. McDermott, shook my hand and congratulated me. I think he respected my work since he was a former Marine. I found the eyes of others upon me in the hallways. Girls who had never spoken to me commented on how much they liked my drawings. It was happening: I was becoming the celebrity I imagined.

Then, just before Thanksgiving, tragedy struck. A mysterious break-in occurred in our art room. Vandals had stolen all of the artwork and speckled blood-red paint over everything, leaving vulgar graffiti behind. Our work was destroyed or gone, except for mine, which remained unscathed in the showcase.

My teacher, Mrs. Strongberger, was beside herself as we cleaned the walls with paint remover and S.O.S. pads. Funding for the art program was running thin and faced a grim future. If budget cuts came, then art class was doomed, and so was her job.

"We're supposed to meet with the selectmen and the school committee tomorrow night," she told us. "What in heaven's name will I do? There's nothing to show them."

Mrs. Strongberger, left with little choice, asked me to be the spokesperson, address the committee about the program, and show my work. A few weeks before, we had been informed that there would be a special guest that night, Congressman Francis "Frankie" Barney, who was an incumbent up for reelection and wanted to demonstrate his awareness of the economy to the precinct. I had heard his name uttered in contempt by my father every morning while he read the *Boston Globe*, but still could not help but think he traveled to Washington D.C., was famous, and that I would address him.

As I walked home in the cold on crooked sidewalks of my small town, I realized that fate had brought me here. I felt an energy, one that would propel me forward to the celebrity I desired. I did not want this feeling to fade.

The next night, Congressman Barney arrived and complimented me on the detail in my artwork; about all the time and effort I must've spent on it. He asked me if I planned to continue to work on art, maybe major in it when I went to college. I told him that I would. My father, who stood in the rear of the meeting room, refused to come up and shake the congressman's hand. And I never took an art class again. By Christmas, our art program was renewed and Frankie Barney won another congressional term.

*

The Machiavellian plan was hatched in my basement over my first cigarette and a can of my old man's Narragansett Beer: I would steal and make the crime scene look legitimate; Mayo would torch the artwork in the woods by the old train tracks, leaving no trace of our malevolence. My remuneration was presenting my artwork to Congressman Barney; Mayo's compensation would be a few packs of my mom's cigarettes and my copies of *Van Halen I* and *II*.

Everything went according to plan, for the most part. I infiltrated the classroom with a key that Mayo had stolen from the custodian after lunch that day. I took three cans of Sherman-Williams scarlet-colored paint out of my gym bag and splattered it everywhere, including on Mrs. Strongberger's desk, even the pictures of her kids. I finished and slipped out the back door, meeting a waiting Mayo on his muddy BMX bike. He pulled up next to me, grabbed the trash bags of art, and gave me the thumbs-up. In his gray-green eyes was an iniquitous look that told me I'd remember this day forever.

I made it home, ate a meatloaf dinner with my family, and went straight to my room. However, Mayo was not so lucky. An elderly neighbor near the old cinder train tracks smelled smoke and investigated. He found Mayo at the scene of the crime, smoking a cigarette and listening to his Walkman as he watched his holocaust of artwork. He never heard the neighbor's footsteps because he had "Runnin' with the Devil" cranked up to maximum volume. The police were called and an investigation ensued. But in the end, Mayo never gave me up.

*

The painting still haunts me weeks after my talk with Mayo on the playground. I begin to dream about the wise man in the blue robe, the one in the middle of *Arabs*. He speaks to me, trying to tell me something in a tongue that I can't discern. I wake every morning wondering what he wants. I prop myself up on my pillows and listen to my son fiddling with his Thomas train set in the playroom and wonder if I should drive to New York, steal back the painting, and return it to its proper spot in my junior high. It could be my penance.

Later, I take my son to his school with his Red Sox back pack and lunch box, give him a kiss, and return to my childhood home to drink coffee and think about his mother, whom I'd left on the West Coast. She loved it so much out there—with *him*—that she decided to walk away from our marriage. I think of her from time to time, but lately the painting seems to block her face in my daydreams in a way that makes the fact that she slept with my closest friend in San Francisco more bearable, less humiliating. My daydream had come true; I had moved to California. But I had lost something important. So had my son.

I wonder how my own mother—two years gone—would feel about my life and the things that I've done. And I wonder how she would feel about our town selling off Juan Pablo Quixote-Santiago's masterpiece. In the afternoons, I read the papers. Between the pages of the small-town rag rages a very public battle, including an outcry from the late donor's family not to sell the painting. A town meeting is announced where townspeople will be allowed to plead their case to bring *Arabs* back from New York. Still, I keep my distance.

I returned to the East for a quiet life and, in my own mind, am bigger than these small-town issues. I've been places, seen things, and moved on from my junior-high self. I don't want to remember what I did. My son will never know. Other than Mayo, the only other person who knows is my ex-wife, whom I told one night at a restaurant in North Beach after too many glasses of Chianti. My secret is safe for now.

*

On the Tuesday before Thanksgiving, Mayo shows up at my house with a six-pack. My son has gone to bed, and we sit drinking beers in the living room.

"So, what are you going to do about that painting?"

"What do you mean?" I reply, after a swig of Sam Adams.

"You gonna go and speak? At least write an Op-Ed for the *Free Press*?"

"I don't think so."

"So, that's it?"

"Yep."

"You ain't gonna save the painting?"

"How can I save it?"

"Speak up. Do something. Challenge it."

"Why would they listen to me?"

Mayo stands up and studies my face. "I'm going to the meeting tomorrow night at town hall," he says. "Are you in?"

"No."

"Fine," he says. "My whole life, it's been about your plans. I'm just going to have to tell them the truth."

He walks to my front door, throws it open, then looks back at me.

"It's wrong what they're doing," he says to me. "I'm a thirty-seven-year-old drunk house painter with no education who has never left this town, and I appreciate that damn painting. Why don't you?"

He slams the door behind him and I am left alone with my thoughts.

*

That night, I have another dream. I am back in San Francisco, down by Fisherman's Wharf looking out toward Alcatraz. It is cold and in the San Francisco Bay I see a man rowing frantically toward the shore. I call out to him as I walk toward the end of the wharf.

"*Hola*," he says. "I am Juan Pablo Quixote-Santiago."

I pull his boat in and moor it to the dock, and reach down and pull him up.

"What are you doing here?" I ask.

"I'm here for my painting, *señor*. I want it back."

"But I don't have your painting."

"Then what is that, *señor?*" he asks, pointing.

I turn to see *Arabs* propped up at the end of the dock. There is a crowd gathered, enamored with the piece. Then, I see Mayo.

"We have to burn it," Mayo shouts, lighting a torch. "We can't leave any evidence."

And next to him is my son. Mayo hands the torch to him and I begin to run toward them. As the flames explode, I awake in my bed to the sound of my son crying. I get up quickly to calm his nightmare. Maybe to calm my own.

*

The next evening, I call my sister to watch my son. I make my way to town hall just minutes before the meeting is to begin. Mayo stands outside, smoking.

"Well, if it isn't our local art aficionado." He smiles, and shakes my hand.

Inside, Mayo sits in the front row, but I begin to make my way to the podium.

"Where are you going? There's a process," Mayo shouts, as I move past the quieted people. All eyes are upon me, some with recognition, others with contempt that I have the audacity to ignore the Puritan by-laws of town assembly. As the lights shine down, I feel like it's the first time since junior high that I've held the attention of a crowd.

"Ladies and Gentlemen," I begin, "I have something to confess to you tonight."

JUST MY IMAGINATION

* * *

When I bought this bookstore, it was my intention to make money off people the same way that booksellers had gouged my pockets for years. It was a lonely, abandoned retail space with whitewashed windows like the shops that Springsteen described on the ghost-ridden boardwalk of Asbury Park in "My Hometown." Main Street in Santa Monica had been forgotten for a while, and I was the benefactor of this recession.

The prior tenant had run a take-out Chinese restaurant here for twenty years and when business slipped, he decided to retire to the Palm Desert with his small fortune gained from orders of Beef Lo Mein, Orange Chicken, and Spring Rolls. He'd leased it from a Jewish landlord named Wolfsheim, a plastic surgeon from Beverly Hills who was simply elated that anyone had taken an interest in the old abandoned space. I'd steered the business through a sluggish economy the first year, but the second year was quite lucrative in a neighborhood filled with screenwriters, actors, and movie-junkies. I began dreaming of joining the rich residents of that "North of Montana Avenue" area, the ones who lived in mansions behind white-picket fences—a pristine neighborhood just blocks from my

❀ ❀ ❀

rent-controlled apartment. My dream seemed to be becoming a reality; I was the proud owner of a store called Cina-Scribe that sold movie scripts.

My wife is a grounded, patient woman, a schoolteacher who politely nods in the same fashion I imagine she does to her students when I come up with these quixotic ideas. First, it was a career as a screenwriter—not exactly a novel idea in Los Angeles. Like others in the mass of expatriate scribes who move to Hollywood, I'd written seven screenplays in my first year in town, scripts about teaching, music, and small-town New England life that I'd once known. She'd read them and agreed they were good, but we both came to realize the politics of the walls that surround Tinseltown and I opted for something a bit more tangible.

I'd read a newspaper article one time about major league baseball players in the old days. They used to buy hardware stores—back home—just in case their careers didn't work out. It was an insurance policy of sorts, in that time following the Great Depression. The future was unpredictable and some made meager salaries, especially the utility guys, not the Mickey Mantle and Ted Williams-types. They were grounded and fearful of God's wrath; the idea of going to the big leagues was nice, but to have a hardware store back home, well that was security. After dealing with Hollywood's unpredictable nature for awhile, I decided to take the same path. But my hardware would be in the form of movie scripts.

Peggy is from the Midwest—Iowa, specifically. She'd grown up on a small farm outside of Des Moines and her family seemed wary of big ideas, especially capitalistic ventures. I'd anticipated this, so when I came up with the idea for the store I had an accounting friend draw up a business plan. Peggy studied the plan for about a week before we took part of our small savings and a business loan, then moved forward with the venture. Peg earned a modest income at a local Christian school and was glad that I'd finally be getting up at a decent hour each morning with her, instead of rising late to sit in front of a keyboard. The rest is history—until Mr. Jangles showed up.

Jangles was a distinguished-looking British man with a propensity for good writing. He'd come to my shop wearing a three-piece navy suit, complete with silver pocket watch and ivory-tipped oak cane. In a strange way, he kind of reminded me of Burt Lancaster when he played the doctor—

Moonlight Graham—in *Field of Dreams*. I would usually be standing behind the counter reading a short story from an anthology and drinking my morning Starbucks when the little silver bell atop my front glass door would announce his arrival. Jangles was articulate, as most of the British are, and he would browse the Newmarket shooting-script editions that had come in with a distinct disdain and offer some aphorism like, "They don't write them like they used to, huh, Lenny?" I'd sip my coffee and reply: "That's right, Mr. Jangles, a worldly scholar of literature like yourself deserves much better."

His story was that he went to Oxford upon the insistence of his military-trained and studied father (he'd fought brazenly on the beaches of D-day) and gotten his degree in four years. Then, Jangles had traveled as a young man, going to places like Paris, Prague, and Rome to write for a few years, before wandering into Russia to study Chekhov in Moscow with the learned scholars. I estimated that he knew no less than six languages. He was a man of tongues.

Trapped behind the cash register for twelve hours a day makes the mind wander—you tend to make up stories. I'd play my own little "escape" games, ones that keep you sane when you're at work. I'd do my reading during downtime and have alternative music constantly playing from some overhead speakers I had installed. Around noon, I'd shut the shop down for an hour to go for a run. The temperate climate of Santa Monica was conducive for me to stay in decent shape all year round and I'd do a loop through Palisades Park, then up the green grassy strips of San Vincente, around the dirt paths of the Brentwood Country Club, to arrive back at the shop. Peg and I installed a small shower and kitchen area in the back, so survival was possible at Cina-Scribe. Lunch was usually at Clif Bar or a takeout from the local Subway. I made it through okay, but the downtime certainly affected my sanity.

But Mr. Jangles was a reliable old friend. He would come by again on his walk in the afternoon and purchase a script or two for his own reading. He seemed obsessed with old scripts like *Casablanca* or *On the Waterfront*, occasionally getting something more cutting edge, like one by Charlie Kaufman.

"I have to hand it to you Americans, Lenny," he'd say. "You invented this art form and when it's brilliant, it's truly brilliant. Literary screenplays can be as well written as any piece of fiction or drama."

I'd nod like an agreeable son and would ring up his purchase, getting him a bag from underneath the counter.

"Don't bother. Save the plastic for someone else, Lenny," he'd tell me.

I'd nod and watch him walk out to the sidewalk and disappear past the Laundromat on Main.

At dinner, Peg would tell me about her day at school, how some pompous parent had handed in their kid's homework after they'd obviously done it for them. She'd talk about the imaginations of her second graders, the fables and stories they'd come up with, the extravagant lies they'd tell. She insisted that no matter how much she focused on morals and ethics, these were habits that would extend far into their adulthood.

"These kids are in the formative stages of their lives and fabrication is all they understand some days," she'd complain. "They need a dose of reality."

"Ah, let them dream," I'd say. "It's natural for kids to make up these stories. Adults need to have a little more of that innocence in them."

"Len," she'd scold, "It's a dangerous habit."

After going on a diatribe or two, she'd clear the dinner table and I'd lie on the couch and watch *The O'Reilly Factor*.

Most nights, Peg would be asleep by nine, tired from her school day—so I'd kiss her sleeping form and wander down to the local pub that my high school friend, Sonny, owned on Wilshire. He'd moved from our hometown in New England ten years before with Hollywood dreams. However, reality set in and he bought the place for a song. It was tangible—something real, something that supported him in a rather Bohemian culture. He'd put up a New England Patriots' banner on a whim and within days the place was packed with overweight expatriated Bostonians—patrons demanding beer and appetizers, both of which he gladly provided.

* * *

I had a stool at the bar, as if I was a cast member of *Cheers*, and even a special mug with my name on it. Sonny would greet me with a smile and shake my hand, congratulating me on my own business success, which was second only to his in Santa Monica. I'd survey the bar, looking for Mr. Jangles, who couldn't resist a dark foamy ale on a warm weeknight. I wished he'd appear so we could talk about some literary things instead of the small talk I was sure to share with the regulars.

It was slow that night, so I got up and selected a few Clash songs off the jukebox as some scantily clad UCLA co-eds laughed and slugged down beers. I found myself thinking about England and the visits I had taken as a young man before I met Peg. I had been a high school English teacher back then and found myself searching for escape from the boredom of my small-town life, desiring a bit of an adventure. Tickets would drop ridiculously low from Boston, $250 for a round trip to Heathrow or Gatwick. I'd go for the week, staying in a little hostel over in Westminster near Kensington Gardens and Princess Di's old castle, backpacking through the Park for hours and reading Shakespeare or Dickens as I sat on the stone lions of Trafalgar across from the National Gallery. Yet, here I was, a middle-aged bookstore owner in California, stuck in a rather mundane existence. I wanted to go to Europe again, travel the world, but my little business held me prisoner. I had sealed my own fate and never considered the repercussions of it all. The Clash song, "Lost in the Supermarket," emanated from the jukebox and made me feel a longing to get away again.

Suddenly, Mr. Jangles appeared beside me. He tipped his hat politely and smiled.

"Good evening, Leonard," he said with a smile.

I nodded to the bartender.

"One for my British friend over here," I said. She shot me a rude look as she studied my half-filled pint, poured another, and set it in front of me.

"What's her problem?" I said to Mr. Jangles.

"Sassy lass," he said with a laugh as he looked away, listening to the music.

"Damn punk music created a bit of havoc in London back in the early '80s. People thought they were part of some kind of a revolution. It was just bloody awful," he said, sipping his pint of London Pride.

* * *

"Wait a second," I interrupted, figuring things in my head. "I thought you were in the U.S. by the eighties, Mr. Jangles," I reminded him suspiciously. He'd often talk about the relevance of the Reagan '80s and how he'd acquired his mansion during that time period.

"I was. Well—that's not totally true. No—I was back and forth for business purposes, you understand," he said, stumbling over parts of his statement.

I turned away for a second, to ease the silence. When I turned back around, Mr. Jangles had disappeared.

That's when I first suspected something was unbalanced with the situation. His story didn't seem to add up; in fact, it was falling apart with every sentence. He suddenly reminded me of some Jay Gatsby type of character, a self-invented man, someone who said only what people wanted to hear, an invention of the mind. I decided to place an investigation of him.

The next week, Jangles came into the shop and bought a couple more scripts, this time *The Sixth Sense* and *Tootsie*, which increased my suspicion. I waited until he exited, letting the bell jingle before twisting the *closed* sign outwards and dashing out the back door through the alley.

I caught sight of him near the 3rd Street Promenade, where he stopped and talked to a homeless man, then checked the time on his pocket watch. Then, he proceeded out across Ocean Boulevard and past The Lobster, and onto the famous pier. I saw him move past the amusement park and Ferris wheel toward the very end of the dock where the Mexican fishermen work and then, as quickly as I found him—he was gone again—disappeared into thin air, vanished like Houdini. All that stood in front of me was the dark, vast Pacific Ocean.

I walked back to Cina-Scribe, bewildered. Was he a magician or illusionist? An escape artist? Or, was he just playing with my mind? I shut down an hour early, had a drink at Sonny's, then walked around the Strand until it started to get dark. I felt as if someone was fooling with my mind.

At dinner that night, I told Peg about the incident with Mr. Jangles and a worried look came upon her Midwest farmer's daughter face.

"I don't think you should be closing the shop during the middle of the day to go on these little adventures of yours," she said angrily.

* * *

Teachers, who are stuck in their restrictive classrooms all day, don't respond well to the mobility of others during their workday.

"Peg, I just want to know who this guy is. He's a good customer. He buys two scripts a day. I'm allowed to check out my customers, right?"

She stared at me with a doubtful look and I decided it was best to just clean the table and wash the dishes. Cleaning helps keep the peace in our house.

Back at the shop the next afternoon, Mr. Jangles arrived on schedule as I was drinking a Red Bull to keep my energy up. He tipped his hat and began browsing the aisles slowly, as if it was first time he'd seen the scripts. I scanned my *L.A. Times* and then looked up at him.

"I followed you yesterday," I finally admitted to him. "I followed you down to the pier, but you disappeared on me."

He stopped for a moment and rubbed his gray mustache with his right thumb and index finger, then looked up at me strangely.

"Followed me—why?" he asked.

"I just wanted to know what your story is—where you lived—where you go each day," I explained. "You're a bit of an enigma to me."

He chuckled and walked toward the counter, tapping his cane against the floor.

"Not the first time I've heard that one, Leonard," he said, amused.

I smiled, hoping there was no ill will, but I wanted to get to the bottom of his character—his story. Who was Mr. Jangles? He rubbed his chin again and tapped his cane rhythmically on the floor.

"Why do I interest you so much? What is it about an elderly British man that is so intriguing to you? You must have many other customers who come in here," he said.

"None as mysterious as you, Mr. Jangles," I admitted.

He placed two new scripts on the counter and smiled at me. It was a copy of *Black Hawk Down* and *The Deer Hunter.*

"Why the violent titles today?" I inquired.

"I like war stories," he related. "As you know, I come from a military—"

• • •

"Family. Yeah, I know."

"Well, tonight, Leonard," he began, "while you're home with that pretty little wife of yours, I'll be reading or perhaps at the movies, far away from here. Just trying to escape for a while."

"Escape what?" I inquired.

"Myself, really. I'm a boring man—an old man. My life is fleeting. It was lived not here, but rather in peaceful exotic lands, where violence and conflict are foreign concepts."

"I don't understand what you're saying," I said frankly.

"Something needs to be done, Leonard. Our existence, our future, the future of the children out there depends on getting people to think, use their heads. Otherwise, communication will cease—and violence and war will ensue. That's what I love about movies and screenplays. If they can convey some of that—well, then, Hollywood ain't so bad."

"I agree," I said with conviction.

"We're in paradise, away from the bombs and chemicals. We're truly fortunate men," he said.

I took his wisdom in, with his sudden surge of philosophical thinking, and rang up his purchase. I handed him the books hesitantly—with a feeling I'd never see him again.

"No plastic, right, Mr. Jangles?" He winked at me, opened the door, and the silver bell announced his exit.

*

When I was a boy, my mother told me later, I had an imaginary friend. His name was Tommy Dolan, the last name coming from a priest who was both family friend and my baptizer. During my first four years, I spent time with Tommy, playing in my backyard and in the nearby woods, entertaining myself with this boy who was like a brother.

When I was older, maybe in high school, my parents revealed to me that during my second year my mother had become pregnant but had lost the baby shortly after birth—they'd kept it from me. They'd named my brother Tommy, and I often wondered if the boy with whom I played was not so much a product of my imagination, but a ghost.

*

After a big dinner one Friday night, I told Peg I'd like to invite Mr. Jangles over for a nightcap. She'd sighed and said that she was tired from her week, but when I insisted she relented and told me to call him.

As I went through the Santa Monica directory, I found no Jangles listed. I called the operator and insisted on the spelling of the man's name, but again there was no listing. After an hour of searching the Internet, I gave up and poured myself a stiff drink and sat and watched some television with my wife. It was a movie—*Memento*—I think. I looked at Peg as her eyelids became heavy.

"I'm tired," she yawned.

I stroked her hair and nodded.

"I'm thinking about closing the shop," I said, picking up my drink and sipping it hard.

She opened her eyes wide and frowned.

"Why? You're just getting going. We're finally making money, aren't we?"

"I just don't want to do it anymore," I said frankly. She nodded, trying to understand.

"And I think I need to see somebody. A psychologist," I continued.

"What's wrong?" she asked, a bit frightened. "Is it this Mr. Jangles?"

I took a hard slug of my drink and set it down on the coffee table, looking away, embarrassed.

"There is no Mr. Jangles," I replied.

BEACH CLUB

I am standing outside of Linc on Melrose, smoking a cigarette. Next to me is a retired swimsuit model named Rhonda, who is scantily clad in one of those red silk over-the-shoulder string blouses. I wear a stupid grin listening to her because I'm drunk and I can't help but think of that Beach Boys' song. It rings in my head as the dry Los Angeles wind blows down upon us and a coyote howls from the hills above Sunset.

Help me, Rhonda. Help, help me, Rhonda...

Rhonda—she's still beautiful—in a celluloid Hollywood, personal trainer, plastic surgery kind of way. And tonight, she is telling me how hard it is for women in California to get married.

"Once you hit thirty, forget it," she says, taking a drag off the Camel that I've given her. "You're done. Dead in the water."

I wonder if she smokes as much as I do ordinarily, or if she's just having a night out after a long day at the beach club. I also wonder if her formula applies to writers out here—over thirty and dead in the water.

"How so?" I ask curiously, amused with her hardship.

"Hey—are you from the Midwest, or something?"

"Boston," I reply. "Small town you've never heard of. We tend to talk funny. Like drunk Kennedys."

"Well," she continues, "the rich forty-something men go for the twenty-something women. Thirty—you're all washed up."

"How old are you?" I wrongfully ask.

"How old do I look?" she says, forcing a sexy smile. She puts her hand to her hip and poses as if she's back on that beach in Maui.

I study her bronze, sun-damaged skin and the wrinkles over her lips. There's been some Botox treatment and perhaps a little plastic surgery. Her breasts have been augmented and enlarged a bit—nothing radical—more of a structural realignment procedure. She is obviously wearing contacts that make her eyes sky blue and her hair is probably styled and colored by a gay German man with a name like Hans who has a salon on or around Rodeo.

"29," I finally blurt.

She frowns and stamps out her cigarette with her red high heel

"You see what I mean?"

"What?"

"I'm 34."

"So, that's good. Right?" I plead defensively.

"Forget it, Teacher-Man from Boston," she says in disgust, patting me on the cheek.

I look through the wide glass window and see my friend Grogan with his high school pal, Huff, uncorking the third bottle of French wine on this impromptu pre-Fourth of July weekend feast. It's Thursday night and I don't have to fly back until Tuesday. I'm supposed to be here to take a look

● ● ●
110

at graduate schools for writing because I think I'm pretty good after getting a story published in a literary journal. Grogan and Huff are laughing about something they find hilarious and I worry for a moment whether I have enough in my bank account to contribute to the $1000 bill.

"Are you going to the beach club this weekend?" retired swimsuit model Rhonda asks me.

"The beach club?" I ask. I think of the graduate schools I'm supposed to visit—the scheduled interviews I've made with deans.

"Yeah," she continues. "Volleyball, Mai Tais, a cookout, fireworks—the whole shebang."

It bothers me for a moment that a drunk, retired swimsuit model named Rhonda says *shebang*. It shouldn't bother me because I'm a high school English teacher, an aspiring screenwriter on a "recruiting" trip, as Grogan, my former college roommate, calls it, out in California. This is Hollywood, a world that people from my small town only know through photographs in *People*, from episodes of *The Hills*, or in the lines of gossip articles on TMZ.com. I think about my wife at home, probably lying on the couch, sleeping while our old television plays. I wonder what she would think of this scene if she could catch a glimpse. She'd either laugh hysterically at its absurdity or be angry as hell. I guess that's the duality that exists in marriage, as well as life. And I guess that's why I find Linc, Rhonda, and Hollywood so fascinating. I'm just a voyeur in this celluloid world.

"So, you are moving out here?" she asks. "Grogie says you want to be a writer." I nod and open the door for her back into Linc.

"Grogie would mention that. Wouldn't he?" I say, embarrassed. "We should really head back in."

I feel flushed as I walk through the crowded dining room as rich people eat their expensive meals in a European backdrop. I'm not sure if it's because of the French wine or the humiliation that I can't afford a dinner roll at Linc. I adjust the green button-down shirt that I bought at an Old Navy in Century City on the way over. I suddenly feel overheated and sit back down at the table, guzzle some ice water, and then nod to the Hispanic waiter for more.

• • •

Grogan looks across at me, his eyes glazed over a bit. He's drunk—with the same intensity that he drank in college. He's an attorney now, looking to become a partner in a year. He's always been extremely generous and has encouraged me to move West to become part of his entourage.

"You okay, Bro?" he shouts, holding up a bottle of the French wine.

"Yeah," I mutter, my face numb from the jet lag, alcohol, and the mesmerizing appearance of Ms. Rhonda—retired swimsuit model.

"More?" he asks, handing the bottle to me.

"Yeah," I say. "More of everything."

*

It's a year later. You've moved to Santa Monica. You tell yourself that you are not the kind of guy who should be a screenwriter. You've actually stood in your full-length bedroom mirror naked and uttered these words. Hollywood is not your type of town. You are from a small town but you came here anyway because you thought you could make it, like thousands of other scribes from across the globe. You now smoke even more cigarettes than you did when you taught, but you also attend spin classes and do yoga. You are overly concerned with your physical appearance and try to network, while sipping protein shakes or Pete's chai tea with agents and actors after your workout. You live in a rent-controlled apartment that should be condemned but is affordable, which is good because you haven't actually gotten paid for anything yet. You spend time wandering Sunset Strip, perusing places like The Viper Room and The Whiskey because you love rock and roll and want to rub elbows with the right people. You do open mics at Best Western in Beverly Hills, just to keep your chops up as a writer.

You don't do drugs—yet. However, if things don't break for you soon, you may be willing to take a sniff of some Columbian marching powder or stick a needle in your arm to ease the pain and anxiety. You think about Michael J. Fox in *Bright Lights, Big City*, and you wonder if you'll follow that character's route while you're out here, do some coke not because you want to make it, but because

hs.

ou grow up?" I ask.

ica," he says. "We had a place on San Vicente."

t did your dad do?"

agent. So was my grandfather. My mother, Mary, was a stepdancer and actress."

e a Bruce Springsteen song," I say. "Just the Hollywood version without the

nancy."

o the chase, Kid," Seamus says to me, reaching into his coat. "I'm in this business

, I feel you have a product here that could make us both really rich, capeesh?"

I reply. "But we've been talking for awhile, and I haven't seen any cash."

me. I am going to get you started because my agency and I believe you can really

ess. The book has sold—we've seen that. Now it's time to look at the big

nat, my agent, Seamus Epstein, sets his checkbook down on the table and I watch

cursively across the bond. He rips it out with one motion and hands it to me. I

$500,000—then slowly look back at him.

ne kind of joke?" I ask.

 an advance to get you started. Get you moved out of that one-bedroom rat-trap

id, right?

ises up his champagne glass and I follow suit. We tap them together and sip.

lon't you, the wife, and the kid come down to our beach club tomorrow? We'll

*

---

you want to forget something very, very sad that happened to you a long time ago. Maybe—you think—an addiction and this memory will make you a better writer, give you an edge, make you more marketable. You read Brett Easton Ellis's novel, *Less Than Zero*, before you came out and so far, even though it's twenty-five years later, he's right on. Your neighbor is even named Clay and is from Sherman Oaks. You came to the City of Angels to hang with the fast crowd, the ones in "The Biz," not the slow one.

You've sold a book. It wasn't a very good book, but it had some interesting short stories that caught the eye of a Beverly Hills agent. He likes one so much that he thinks it might make a good film and commissions you to write the screenplay, which qualifies you as a screenwriter. He tells you to meet him at The Polo Room one night to sign the papers. You're not one to fool around with opportunity, so you hail a cab for the Beverly Hills Hotel and arrive fifteen minutes early.

*

The hotel is lit up, displaying its pink exterior, and I feel important as I stride into the bar. Hotel security approaches me, but my agent steps in and pushes him aside.

"He's okay," says Seamus Epstein, the first Irish Jew to take over Hollywood's elite agency: ES—Emerald Star. "He's a writer. He's with me."

The large security guard steps aside and I shake hands with my agent.

"Have a seat over here," he says. "You bring your wife?"

"No."

"Well, you could've brought her. Bring her next time. She'd probably like this place. My wife loves it."

I decide I will not to tell my wife about his invitation. She's at home with the baby, probably struggling to get him to sleep. She wouldn't appreciate such a missed opportunity.

"So—the collection. I read it again," Seamus begins. "Absolutely love it, Babe. As you know, I have family from Dorchester. That's the Irish side. The Jews are out here."

I nod and sip a glass of champagne that has been set in front of me. I feel no challenge to my masculinity that a Jewish-Irish agent calls me *babe*. The champagne is bitter because it's expensive; I gag, but somehow manage not to spit it out on him.

"I like the way you refused to follow a linear path in any of the stories. The narrative goes back and forth like a pendulum. Seems like a dream—very surreal—very Christopher Nolan. Very fucking cinematic, Babe."

So we are swearing tonight. Excellent. I like a man with an edge, especially if he is negotiating deals on my behalf.

"I've got two actors who want to do something with that story, 'Hibernians,'" he says. "The one about the kid going back to his uncle's funeral."

"Ancient Hibernians," I correct him. "Kind of autobiographical."

"Well, you want names?"

"Absolutely," I reply, downing the rest of champagne. It tingles in my stomach. I want more. More of everything.

"Luke Wilson and Keanu Reeves," he says, waiting for my reaction.

I look at him incredulously.

"Aren't they kind of…"

"Old?" he says, before me. "Yeah—abso-fucking-lutely, Babe. But how old are you?"

"28."

"And the character?"

"Gabriel is supposed to be 27."

He nods and taps his fingers together as if he's getting ready to say an Our Father, which is unlikely because he's mostly Jewish, which is more powerful than Irish in Hollywood, unless you're making a film about the Boston Mob. He nods and then points at me as if he's had an epiphany.

"Make-up will take care of that. Plus, those two are skinny little bastards and that makes them look younger, too," he says finally. "But don't worry about casting. Let's worry about a number that will make us both very wealthy."

"Fine with me," I say, smiling. "But, let's around with 'Ancient Hibernians'."

"Come again?"

"I said I don't want to mess with it. It's a Quentin Tarantino or Kevin Smith getting a hold of

"Who do you think you are, Babe? J.D. Sa

I laugh and champagne trickles out my no BHH monogrammed on it in pink.

"And, by the way, I like Kevin Smith," m

"Me too. But not for this story," I say, as Howard or Wes Anderson piece."

My agent looks around the Polo Room as real client like Vince from *Entourage* or a female cast

"You're a bright kid—bright boy," he beg

"That's what they told me at USC."

"Yeah, well, they let my cousin's half-reta be so confident. The right person donates on your

"Gee, thanks, but my folks didn't donate. Eight-point-two-percent interest on that loan."

"And remind me, what were you doing b

"I was a high school English teacher. And

"Opinion column?"

"That's right."

My agent smiles as if he's recalling his ow comes over. He orders a cheese plate and some app

"How much did that opinion column pay

"Nothing. I did it for free. Hometown thi

It's a year earlier, two days after our lavish dinner at Linc. I'm at the beach club sitting next to Rhonda and Grogan, watching a skydiver land in the middle of the sandy volleyball court. The crowd roars as he waves an American flag in his descent. It's the Fourth of July.

"Nice recruiting trip, huh?" shouts Grogan.

I nod and sip my Mai Tai. The sun feels good. The place is packed. Rhonda doesn't look so retired in her two-piece bikini.

I've missed my meetings with the deans and directors. My wife would kill me if she knew. Grogan promises to make some phone calls on my behalf. As an attorney, he assures me he has solid connections in L.A.

"So what's your novel about?" asks Rhonda, as the volleyball game begins again. It's the semifinals. The players are club members but Karch Kiraly and Syngin Smith are the ringers, with a few Olympic gold medals between them.

"It's not a novel. It's a collection of short stories, and it's not done yet."

"That's interesting. Did I ever tell you my first husband was a writer?" shares Rhonda.

"Really?" I say, sipping some more of my Mai Tai. I hate it. I think a beer would taste better than this concoction.

"Yep. He wrote screenplays. Sold four or five," she says.

"Wow."

"He lives in Pittsburgh now."

"Huh?"

"Last I heard, he was working in a supermarket. Stock boy. Stamps the cans."

I nod and wonder how much truth is in her story. If you use the Hollywood formula, it's probably about fifty-percent true.

Grogan nods to me and I get up and follow him out to the bar. I set down my Mai Tai and let the dizziness sink in. I feel good, like I've escaped something, but Rhonda's story about the stock boy screenwriter bothers me.

* * *

"So, this is a pretty nice life," says Grogan, ordering us two beers. "Isn't a bad view, huh?"

He points out to the sandy beach where the Heineken girls are doing a promo between sets.

"Not bad, Buddy."

"So, you coming out?"

I laugh. Grogan has been asking me that since sophomore year in college. He was the first guy I met at college, choosing a cold Catholic university 3,000 miles from this very point where he grew up just above us in the Palisades.

"It looks good," I reply. "Things could happen for me out here. I feel good."

Grogan throws his arm around me.

"Come on," he says. "Let's take a couple of beach cruisers and head up to Bel Air Bay. The fireworks will be coming up afterwards."

I smile and raise my beer.

"To success," I say. "And a little money."

"No," says Grogan. "A shit load of money."

I beam and tap his glass.

*

You're back from your historic meeting with your Beverly Hills agent. You hesitate at your apartment door because it's past midnight and you know your wife has just gone to sleep after another late-night feeding of your infant son. However, what's in your pocket can magically make all of the pain go away. It can stop the arguments about how you waste time writing in coffee shops or talking to your writer friends on the phone. It can make the credit card debt with your tuition payments disappear. It can make the cost of daycare vanish and replace it with a full-time Mexican nanny named Consuelo. It can make those drives you've taken up past the school you teach at in the Palisades on Sundays legitimate. It can make those open houses more than just tours of homes you'll never own.

What's in your pocket is magic, and your fingertips dancing on a dirty laptop keyboard created it. For a moment, you consider yourself a wizard.

But then sobriety sets in. What if the check isn't real? What if you've just handed over all the rights to your intellectual property to an Irish-Jew agent? You think of Leopold Bloom from *Ulysses*. He tried to help Stephen Dedalus, didn't he? But like the mythological allusion of that novel, this whole venture has been an Icarian dream. Your father told you not to go to Los Angeles. He pouted for two weeks, actually, because you were not following the plan, his plan, the one that put you in the house with the two kids, two cars, and the mortgage. The one that he labored to maintain while you pursued your sports and your writing. But you shunned it and headed West. Now, you have a son and responsibilities. And this thing in your pocket, this green bond of currency allegedly worth half-a-million dollars, is going to make all those responsibilities seem a more manageable.

You put your key in and turn the knob. The door creaks open and you walk in on tiptoes. You take the check out and set it on the table, half-folded next to the ceramic change jar and pile of unpaid bills and parking tickets. You walk down the hall to your son's room and study his sleeping form in his crib for a moment, before your wife calls out.

"Who's there?" she asks.

You pause for a moment, then walk into the dark bedroom.

"Just me," you say, as you click off the hallway light.

*

I drive my used Volvo wagon up Chataqua. My wife is sitting next to me, holding my hand, and I smile and glance back at my son who is in his car seat in the back. We are one happy American family. We are going to look at houses—in the Palisades.

"What's the Realtor's name, again?" my wife inquires.

"Rhonda—something," I reply.

"Oh," she laughs. "Like the Beach Boys' song."

"Yeah," I reply with a nod. "She's a friend of Grogan's. I've only met her like—twice."

"Oh, a friend," my wife says, using her fingers as quotation marks.

We are looking at properties on the Alphabet Streets. Smaller homes still in the $1 million range far away from the palatial mansions that Tom Hanks and Kobe Bryant own. Seamus's advance was a nice down payment, but we're going to need some more revenue from "Ancient Hibernians." Wahlberg now wants to direct, so another advance is possible. There's been a bidding war on the screenplay. The British kid from the vampire movie has expressed interest in playing the lead role.

"If things work out," I begin, "I think I'd like to get an Audi."

"An Audi wagon?"

"I was thinking a convertible. A black one."

"My son is not riding in a convertible," my wife interjects.

"Okay, okay," I say defensively. "Just an idea."

"There's smog and projectiles," she exclaims. "Drive-bys."

"We live in Santa Monica, not Compton."

"You weren't out here in 1998," she reminds me. "Five people gunned down in a week!"

We pull up in front of the small white house on L Street. I get out and my wife takes my son out of his car seat. He looks curiously at the house as if it's a spaceship landed on Earth. After living in an apartment for a while, I feel the same way. Rhonda walks up looking like she's a model in the Talbot's catalogue: blue blazer, skirt, white silk blouse.

"Hi, Rhonda," I say nervously.

"This must be your lovely wife," she says, sticking out her hand. "I've heard so much about you."

"Oh—thank you," says my wife, looking at me curiously. I shrug and take my son into my arms.

"Shall we take a look inside?" asks Rhonda. I'm a bit shocked by her professionalism.

We walk into the house. It's perfect, all done over: stainless steel everything in the kitchen. There's a playroom for the baby. There are three bedrooms total, a backyard with a small pool, a mudroom, a breakfast nook, a dining room. Our apartment down below in Santa Monica seems dwarfed by the space here.

"So, what do you think?" asks Rhonda.

"I love it," my wife blurts. She turns to me. "Right, Honey?"

"Yeah," I say. "Right."

"Well, let's go back to the office and make an offer, if you're ready," says Rhonda. I nod and we walk out to the front lawn. My wife puts my son in the car and gets in. I look back at Rhonda, who squints at me.

"Can you afford this?" she says scornfully. I look at her dumbfounded and nod.

"Yeah."

"Are you sure? I thought you were a teacher."

"I recently came into some money," I whisper. She stares at me, then nods.

"Fine," she says. "But I have a reputation to uphold."

I watch her walk toward her Mercedes on the corner of L Street and think about our day at the beach club the year before.

*

I am sitting in my family's cabana at the beach club on a Saturday in August. I'm with my wife and son, just lounging in the sand, discussing private preschool and renovations to our new home. My Blackberry vibrates. I look at the screen and see that it's Seamus.

"What's up, Babe?" he begins.

"Not much," I say. "Just relaxing at the beach club."

"Yeah, right," he replies anxiously.

"Anything wrong?" I ask, feeling a pit in my stomach.

"The project's been shelved."

"Shelved?"

"Yeah, Babe," he says. "HBO just signed Walberg for a couple more seasons of *Entourage*. He's very busy."

"Right," I say. "So, that's it."

"That's it," Seamus says softly. "For a while. I'm not saying for good, Babe."

"Right," I say, not believing him.

I nod and hang up the phone. I rehearse what I'll say to my wife, something about how it will all be okay. Something about how living in a small town back in Massachusetts isn't such a bad thing, and it's truly where our son should grow up anyway.

I look around the beach club, studying the sand and bright blue ocean in front of us, but can only think of the Palm Desert for some reason. The cool sea breeze has died down and I feel hot, then wonder how long it will be until they kick us out for not paying our dues. Suddenly, I remember that today is my birthday. I am thirty and thirty is too old to be a screenwriter in Hollywood.

TRACKS

The vision was so vivid that Gus was sure it had to be real—this was definitely not a dream. In fact, he was positive it was happening, for there were too many verifiable qualities. He felt the vibrant sun shining down against his aging face and the dew from the wet grass beneath his bare feet. The blades flattened as he walked forward, scrunching beneath his dampened toes. He heard the birds chirp from the bordering arboretum. It was all occurring in real time, real-life, but at the same time—it felt surreal. Gus pinched himself on the arm just to make sure, and felt the sharp pain through his red silk pajamas.

As he stood in the pristine field, Gus observed a huddled figure in the distance—a man sitting in a blue lawn chair with a guitar fixed in his hands, strumming away. He heard the vibrant chords of "Strawberry Fields Forever" emanating acoustically, and began walking toward the man ever-so-slowly across the trim grass. He heard a voice over the music, echoing into nature like the sweet scent of roses, resonating melodically off the surrounding trees, drifting brightly into the air. It was a sad and soft voice, a bit gravely from cigarette smoking—but familiar to him. For all the times Gus had heard this Beatles' tune, it had not sounded so lachrymose—like a young man singing a funeral hymn.

* * *

About halfway there, Gus began to change his mind about the reality of the scene—he started to wonder if this was in fact not a dream, but—heaven.

Still, he continued, and, at the edge of the field, noticed an English-style garden with ripe fruit growing from verdant trees and bushes. As he passed, he picked a plump strawberry from a vine and bit into it. It was fresh and sweet and he savored its luscious flavor. If he wasn't in heaven, perhaps this was the Garden of Eden, he thought.

As Gus arrived at the figure in the chair, he saw a man in his twenties clad in a leather jacket, white T-shirt, worn blue jeans, his longish brown hair slicked back. It was John Lennon, looking much like his younger Hamburg Beatle years. Adrenaline ran through Gus's body and he attempted to speak, but nothing came out. It was as if his voice had been stolen, his vocal chords paralyzed.

"Look to what they've thrown away, Mate," said Lennon, smiling a bit. "The kids, Gus—they'll carry on what we've started here."

Lennon held up a peace sign and smiled. Gus shook his head and shrugged to show that he didn't understand.

"The tapes—mate. You have to find those tapes," said Lennon, pushing back his greased hair with his hand.

Then, without warning, thunder crashed and a fresh gunshot wound appeared in Lennon's chest. He stopped playing and looked down, then smiled sadly, helplessly, almost resigned to the fact that something like this was bound to happen. He struggled to lean forward, then dropped the guitar into his lap and put his hand to his chest, instinctively trying to stop the blood from flowing out of him. Gus knelt down to assuage his pain, but Lennon waved him off.

"It's just me bloody fate."

"I'm a doctor," Gus cried. "I can help you."

But Lennon held up his hand firmly for Gus to stop. "It's just me time to go, Gus. I'll see you on the other side of things, then," he said in his Liverpool working-class accent.

And without warning, Lennon went through a metamorphosis, changing into a teenage girl with long brown hair, dark circles under her eyes, and a razor blade in her hand. Snakes followed her as she walked toward a horrified Gus. She held the razor dangerously close to her wrists, then swiftly cut both and held them up proudly. Blood dripped down her arms and her lips moved into a depraved smile. Gus stood up from his kneeling position and backed away in horror.

"No!" he screamed.

"Dr. Spectra, I warned you. You wouldn't listen to me," she whispered to him. "I warned you about this."

And then—

Darkness.

*

As Gus awoke in his mundane room, he realized that as quickly as the surreal images had arrived, they had disappeared—it had all been a dream. He sat up quickly and felt his heart racing, and began looking around to establish his bearings. There was only darkness around him—no English garden, no John Lennon, no green field, no music, no teenage girl, no visible wounds to heal.

His brain had been working overtime these days. Gus got out of bed slowly, felt the beads of sweat on his forehead and the dampness in his long gray beard. He stared at the glowing red numbers on his alarm clock, saw that it was 4:30 a.m., and shook his head. Wiping his face with a bath towel from his dresser, he descended the creaky steps of his house and walked zombie-like into the kitchen.

The dream didn't make sense. Lennon had died when he was forty, not twenty, as the young man had looked in his dream. And why would he have such an awful nightmare? The girl—well, she had been bad luck. He'd been forced to take the fall for the hospital and, in many ways, knew he had been set up.

Gus set up his coffeemaker and grabbed his pack of Camels, heading to the back porch for an early dawn smoke. He studied the lights of Providence lingering in the skyline. It occurred to him that he was not in heaven, but that didn't stop him from feeling dead inside.

It had been six months since the trial and his termination from Charles Berry Memorial Hospital, where he had practiced adolescent psychology for the last twenty years. He had helped many kids get back on their feet after bouts of depression, suicide attempts, as well as struggles with sexual and substance abuse. He had been a healer, a popular psychologist among the troubled youth, the man with a veritable reputation whom everyone turned to when their kids needed counseling. They had called him Dr. Angus Spectra or Dr. Gus then, but today he was a man without a professional title. He was a beleaguered man indicted and convicted of the worst possible crime in medicine: temerity. They had crucified him in fewer than two weeks in a New Bedford courtroom, accused him of recklessness, stripped him of his life, his reputation, and tossed him out into the mean streets. Now, he was just a scared, unemployed, middle-aged man who had strange dreams and spent his days wondering how he was going to make his mortgage payments, pay alimony based on a salary he didn't have anymore, and send his son to college. He finished his cigarette and threw it in an old Folgers coffee can filled with dirty rain water. It was Saturday. He needed to occupy himself—focus on his new obsession.

Gus went back to the kitchen and poured himself a cup of coffee, then booted up his old computer to look at Craigslist. It seemed that ever since he'd lost his license to practice psychology in the state of Massachusetts, he'd developed a strange affinity for yard sales. He'd roam from town to town like a gypsy, searching for something unique and valuable to buy. Although he was still a neophyte, he felt himself improving with each experience, each new sale, developing a professional eye for antique items in the same way he had come to understand his patients and solve their problems. He was like Odysseus wandering from island to island, trying to find his way back to Ithaca, collecting treasures along the way, trying to reestablish his identity. In fact, the scraggy gray beard that Gus maintained made him look quite like the Greek king at the end of *The Odyssey*. He had started to grow it after the trial as a sign of his departure from the professional world and he vowed not to shave until he was absolved. But he knew deep down that his mission to exonerate himself was a rather hopeless one, and that he would most likely live out his days never seeing his old office and leather lounge couch again.

He was up early today and decided to plot his assault on suburbia by printing out a few ads. He sipped his coffee and meandered through the links, trying to distinguish between the true yard sales and the fraudulent ones where the people would create the façade that their driveway or garage, like ancient merchants in Venice or Rome, actually held something salable. It was suburban chicanery, a waste of his time and the time of other serious collectors. There were other people who would line their driveways with used and melted Tupperware containers of all shapes and sizes, broken television sets and toaster ovens, and racks and racks of moth-eaten Goodwill fare. Others would stack dusty and dented furniture and contorted mattresses from their back rooms and basements in hope that some young newlywed couple or college student would come and pay something for their junk. Like a navigator plotting his nautical route, Gus had his plan for the morning by the time he polished off his second cup of coffee. He'd wake his son, Dusty, for track practice, then head out on the roads for his day.

But the thing was, as trivial as the yard sales seemed in comparison to psychology, Gus just loved the feeling of sifting through people's junk. He liked to study their oldest and most dear possessions—the ones that must have meant enough to them that they struggled with the thought of finally letting go. He'd often repeat the old cliché to himself: "One man's trash is another man's treasure." And it was true, for he had made a meager living off eBay, selling old records, instruments, and antiques, anything of value. The money was okay but it was the art of searching, seeking, sifting through the possessions of others that made him feel good.

Around seven, he got dressed, woke Dusty for practice, and headed out to the '93 Saab he had purchased with the winnings from the Braverman Award for Adolescent Psychology just nine years ago. The car desperately needed some work, like a new exhaust system. As he turned the key, the whole garage vibrated from the roaring noise of the engine. He backed down the drive and headed south to Borough, a small town on the Rhode Island border that had been slowly gaining a reputation as the next up-and-coming community.

He stuck a Beatles' tape in his cassette player and turned it up to drown out the loud muffler. The tape was a bit slow and distorted from years of repeated play but it still sounded good to him, like a scratched old record on a turntable, and the music helped him pass the time. Gus saw himself as a survivor, like McCartney and Ringo, the two living members of the Fab Four. He knew that he'd have to cut out the smokes if he didn't want to end up like George, and he didn't have any worries about going the way John did—he wasn't famous enough. Still, he'd endured hardship: a divorce, paying alimony from his life savings, the girl's parents' lawsuit, a brief cocaine addiction, a thirty-year smoking habit. But he viewed his trials as tests he had passed through along the way. He was stalwart; there was no denying that. He stuck another Camel in his mouth and lit it, turning up "Here Comes The Sun," focusing on the guitar solo.

What was it about John Lennon that made Gus dream of him? Perhaps it went back to his youth, when he saw them on the *Ed Sullivan Show*. Maybe it was the energy they had created, particularly with women. He'd shared an appreciation for the band with his ex-wife, before things had gone bad. But there was something more to his affinity with Lennon—nothing short of a riddle or labyrinth.

Gus drove around the wealthy neighborhoods of Borough, looking at each yard sale offered by the palatial mansions. He spent an hour pulling up to and past driveways, surveying the goods of the rich, but there was nothing: it was all useless junk. An Oriental rug salesman tried to sell his small samples for ridiculous prices, a Mary Kay guru had lipstick and mascara for sale on her tables, and a retired pro football player had lined his lawn with various pieces of equipment and used turf shoes for fans to buy. There was nothing of value for Gus. He drove to Dunkin' Donuts for his fourth coffee of the morning and headed to the other side of town—the factory side of old Borough.

Borough in Gus's mind was not that different from a small village in England. As he passed the industrial zone of his town, he imagined it to be not that different from a neighborhood in Liverpool. There were brick row houses, the kind you'd find in the city. This had been a section where, back in the 1800s, the Irish had immigrated in order to work in the jewelry factories like his Italian ancestors. There was a sense of resilience here, the red-brown faces of the buildings defiant against the troubles of the world. This defiance seemed to have bled into the souls of the immigrants, and it was as if they became the personification of these façades—aware that life was full of heartbreak and

* * *

130

obstacles. Gus tried to become like them with his approach—he needed to be strong for himself and his son if he ever wanted to redeem his name and his profession in this town.

Gus pulled the Saab over and checked his paper, seeing that there was a sale off Main Street in a neighborhood of former jewelry factory owners' homes. He finally found the old white Victorian and parked the car on the street. He put on his black sunglasses and walked up the driveway to a series of card tables showcasing a plethora of junk. His face was close enough to the front page of the *Borough Times* that someone might recognize him as "that psychologist."

Lining the stone walls and blankets near the driveway was a green rotary dial telephone from the '70s, some old family silverware, religious items, the board game Monopoly, ice skates, old shoes. He studied the items for a minute or two and sighed. There seemed to be nothing for him today. For a moment he contemplated leaving, but looked up to see an old man, obviously the owner of the Victorian, watering his yellow, burnt lawn with a green garden hose. He wore a yellow cardigan, blue Bermuda slacks, and a Red Sox hat, and waved to him. He reminded Gus of his deceased father, who loved the Red Sox and struggled to maintain his own lawn up to his death.

"Lawns are a challenge to keep up, huh?" Gus shouted sympathetically to the man.

The old man shut off the hose and nodded.

"If you don't care for them, they'll just burn themselves to death," shouted back the old man.

"Years of work. They need a lot of nurturing," Gus shouted. "You should try ChemLawn."

"Nah, I do it the old-fashioned way," responded the man as he went back to his hand watering. "No chemicals. Just water, fertilizer, and hard work."

Gus smiled, and then continued down the driveway toward the garage when something caught his eye: a stack of old records. As he thumbed through them, a woman in her seventies approached him.

"Oh—do you like music, young man?" she asked curiously, as her wrinkled face brightened.

"Young man?" he laughed. "Yes, Ma'am, very much. How much are these?" Gus asked. He'd be fifty in three weeks.

"Well, why don't you have a look through and we'll see what you pick out," she said kindly, moving on to another customer who was looking at an old dresser.

He spent a few minutes going through the stacks and selected some decent records, twenty in all. There was *Beggars Banquet*, *Pet Sounds*, *Revolver*, *Sgt. Pepper's Lonely Hearts Club Band*, *The White Album*, *Exile on Main St.*, *London Calling*, *Rubber Soul*, and *Who's Next*, all in decent condition, all vinyl. He'd finally found some treasures in all of his wandering.

"Do you realize you have *Rolling Stone* magazine's top 100 albums of all-time here?" he commented, trying to sound impressed.

"Those were my son's records. He left them behind," she said, frowning.

"Oh, has he moved away?"

"He's quite ill, actually."

"I'm sorry," said Gus, embarrassed by his invasiveness.

"Do you like the albums?" said the old woman, maneuvering around the awkward moment.

"Very much. How much can I give you for them?"

She did some calculation in her head and looked down.

"Will you use them?"

"Excuse me?"

"I said, 'Will you use them?' Will you listen to the records?"

Gus looked at her strangely.

"Of course. I have an old record player in my basement. Belonged to my grandfather. I'll take very good care of them," he lied. He knew that he would most likely sell them on the Internet—probably keep a couple for himself. Every little bit of money helped.

She paused again and looked him in the eye.

"You seem like a nice, trustworthy young man. Why don't you just take them? Just promise me you'll listen to them."

Gus nodded and reached in his pocket, taking out some cash. He was uncomfortable with such charity. He didn't want to owe anyone anything.

* * *

"Listen, I'm a collector, so why don't I give you five dollars an album? There are twenty here, so here's a hundred dollars. These records still have some value."

He handed her a wad of cash, but she waved him off.

"Please, it would mean a lot to me and my husband."

Gus looked at her husband still watering the yellow lawn, and nodded to him. The old man waved back and turned to spray some water on his dying plants. Gus saw that the old lady was not willing to debate.

"Okay. Thank you. Thank you very much, Ma'am."

He put the stack of albums under his arm, turned, and walked back towards his old red Saab, curious as to why she turned his money down, but respectful enough not to pry. There was more to the story of these records and he knew it. Just as he opened his car door, the old woman shouted from the burnt lawn.

"Sir, did I hear you say you are a collector?"

Gus set the records down in the front seat of the car and looked up, confused.

"Yes, I am," he shouted back.

She waved for him to come toward the house.

"Why don't you come in for a second? I'd like for you to see something."

He followed her up the brick steps into the old Victorian, and they descended into the finished basement, which smelled of mildew and old cigarette smoke. They squeezed around boxes marked *Christmas and Easter Decorations*, and went into a back room. Gus stood in awe. There was a Fender electric guitar, a Roland keyboard, a Fender jazz bass, an Alesis drum machine, and some sort of Tascam recording device with earphones attached. She pointed to the items.

"Would you be interested in any of these?" she asked.

Gus surveyed the situation. Everything was dusty, as if it had not been used in a long time. It looked like a graveyard of musical instruments, as if a band had just gotten up from the studio one day, walked out, and never returned. The instruments looked nice and he knew that they would be worth something, either on eBay or at a pawnshop. But, it was the recorder that interested him the most. He sat down in front of it and fiddled with the colorful knobs and buttons.

"I like this one. It looks like a vintage old four-track like the Beatles might have used," he said. The old woman smiled nostalgically.

"You're welcome to take whatever you like," she whispered.

Gus looked at her. Why did she want to get rid of all this equipment so badly?

"Listen, Ma'am. I'd have to give you some money for these items. I'm not going to lie to you. This could sell in a music shop for a few hundred dollars," he said.
She nodded.

"But, I'll know they're in good hands if you take them," she replied. "You're not some greedy pawnshop owner who'd try to take advantage of me. Are you?"

He looked at her old, wrinkled face, and shook his head.

"I couldn't accept all these," he said, feeling guilty.

"Well, how about just the recorder? You seem to like that," the old woman said. "And here are some tapes that go with it."

She handed him a box of old cassette tapes. "Please, it would mean a lot to me and my husband," she pleaded.

Gus nodded and got up.

"Okay, I'll take the recorder, but if you're going to get rid of the other instruments," he said, as he walked up the steps, "I want you to get some real money for them."

*

Gus drove home thinking about the dusty and abandoned basement, the instruments, and the kind old woman. He brought the recorder down to his own basement and cleared the tools off his dormant workbench and set up the device like a kid putting together a Christmas present. This, he thought, would be his new long-term project. There was no manual and he had no knowledge of how the damn thing worked. These were all the pieces of the perfect puzzle he'd have to put back together.

He stuck in one of the cassette tapes, put on a pair of old earphones, and clicked the "play" button. Then came one of the strangest symphony of discordant sounds he had ever heard. It was eerie, a haunting, slow beat of drums coming every three or four seconds, and a distorted voice singing slowly, like the kind used in horror movies. It made him sit up straight, and a chill ran down his spine. *What the hell is this?*

He clicked the "stop" button and felt his heart beating hard. Then, he fiddled with the knobs and buttons for the next few hours, before finally giving up for the night. It was beyond his skill. He went upstairs and located Dusty, who was working in his room on his computer.

"Hey, Dusty," he said.

"Hi, Dad."

"Listen, can you take a look at the recorder I got today? Fiddle around with it. See if you can get it to play properly. Right now, it sounds like a melting tape."

Dusty, a bit annoyed, preoccupied with a conversation on Facebook, nodded without turning around.

"Sure, Dad. I'll check it out. Later."

Gus nodded and closed the door. He knew his son thought he was a loser for what had happened; the kids surely talked at school. Maybe this recorder was a way he could earn his trust again. He walked down the hall and collapsed on his bed. It had been a long and eventful day. He said a prayer for the old lady and her sick son as he drifted off.

*

Gus stood staring out at the emerald-green Mediterranean Sea. He was in Monaco, on a yacht, looking toward Monte Carlo, drinking a martini and soaking up the sun. John Lennon came on deck and sat down beside him.

"Well—Gussie-Boy," he said with a smile. "You found some treasure?"

"Yeah. I found those tapes you told me about."

"Good, bloody good!" said Lennon, lighting a cigarette. "Now all you have to do is figure them out."

Gus looked at him, confused.

"Figure what out?" he asked. "Can't I just enjoy them?"

"Nah—that's too easy, Mate," replied Lennon. "Everything I wrote was a riddle. McCartney was into that "Love Me Do" bollocks. Not me, Gus!"

He stood up and looked at the water.

"Catch you later, Gussie-Boy," said Lennon, as he dove into the sea.

*

Suddenly, he heard his son's voice calling with urgency: "Dad, Dad, Dad..."

"Dad, wake up. Wake up."

Gus sat up quickly. Dusty looked at him with crazed eyes, and shook him hard.

"What, what's wrong?" Gus blurted sleepily.

"Come downstairs. You've got to hear this."

"Now?" he asked, staring at the red digits on the clock. It was 3:30 a.m.

"Now, Dad. Let's go. You gotta hear this."

Gus got out of bed slowly, the feeling reminding him of when a patient called in the middle of the night for an emergency. He hadn't been an MD, but was on call 24/7. The girl had called him at home the night she had hurt herself, and he had staggered out of bed to talk with her. But she didn't really want to talk; she had already made up her mind.

"Dr. Spectra, I warned you. You wouldn't listen to me," she whispered to him. "I warned you about this."

He had been drinking that night—Scotch, actually. He had hastily made his way out to the garage and gotten into the Saab. About two miles from the hospital a deer had wandered into the road and he had gone off, into a ditch. By the time he'd gotten the car back on the road and arrived at Charles Berry Memorial Hospital, the girl was dead. That's when the inquiries started—when it all came out.

He slung on his old blue bathrobe and followed his son down the creaky steps to the basement workbench as Dusty ran to the recorder, which was now attached to an old Sony boom box, a plethora of red, yellow, and white cords running into it for external monitoring.

"Are you ready?" his son said with a proud and excited voice.

Gus nodded groggily.

"Did you fix it?" Gus asked, yawning.

"It wasn't broken, Dad. The effect knob was just on a slower speed. It has to be up here at twelve o' clock to play correctly." He pointed to the recorder's positioning.

"Well, I'm glad I'm not a doctor anymore, or I'd feel stupid," he replied, lighting a Camel and blowing the smoke out under the fluorescent lights. Dusty clicked "play" and there was a pause.

Then, there was a symphony of rock-and-roll pouring forth from the beat-up boom box. Gus sat up in his seat, his cigarette falling to the floor, his jaw dropping wide open. He heard the vibrant chords emanating outward and the voice over them, echoing in his basement like the sweet scent of roses, resonating melodically off the concrete walls, drifting brightly into the air. It was a sad, but passionate male voice rising up above the raw electric guitar and melodic keyboards. It was a voice like many Gus had heard before—like Jagger, Westerberg, Bono—but unique. It was the best rock-and-roll sound he had heard in his fifty years. Perhaps, the best music he had ever heard.

"What the hell is this? Who is this? " he muttered.

Dusty shook his head.

"I don't know. I mean, it's not exactly my kind of music. But it's good. Real good. Kind of like that Lennon guy or Kurt Cobain, or something. The music behind it, it's just blended perfectly. It sounds awesome. Where did you get this?"

Gus stood up and fiddled with the knobs.

"At a yard sale," he whispered.

"Well, the tape you played was set at a slow speed for recording. These are all master tapes that can only be played in the recorder to sound right. Then, you have to mix it down to a normal cassette tape after getting the levels right," said Dusty.

Gus stared at the machine, the tapes, and then back at his son. Whoever had created these tapes was some kind of musical genius, and he needed to find him.

*

Gus arrived at the old Victorian house the next morning. He felt a bit sluggish from his early wake-up call, but nevertheless approached the walkway that ran between the dying rose bushes and burnt lawn. He rang the bell and looked around. After a moment, the old woman came to the door and smiled.

"How are you!" she said cheerfully. "You're the gentleman from the yard sale the other day. Won't you come in?"

She opened the door and invited him into a living room whose furniture was covered in plastic. Gus sat on the flowered sofa and the old woman brought in a tray of tea and cookies from the kitchen.

"So, Mr.—?"

"My name is Spectra—Gus Spectra."

"Yes, Mr. Spectra. Did you change your mind about the guitars and other items downstairs?"

Gus frowned and looked around the room. There were pictures of the old woman and her husband on beaches, in the mountains, in Europe, and he studied them closely, looking for evidence of their son.

"I'm here to talk to you about the recorder and those tapes you gave me."

The woman nodded.

"Is it working okay? I don't like to give people junk, you know."

"It's working fine, Ma'am. It's just that my son and I were listening to the tapes in our basement the other night and we'd like to meet the singer on them. He's fantastic."

The old woman frowned back at him.

"I'm sorry, Mr. Spectra. That's just not possible. My son is ill."

Gus nodded politely as the old woman shifted in her seat against the plastic. There was an awkward silence and the grandfather clock ticked loudly enough for Gus to hear it. He studied an old piano that sat beneath the stairwell and took a deep breath.

"Do you play?"

The woman nodded. "I played when I was younger, when I had time. It was my father's piano. He was a singer—amateur, you understand. He sang at church and variety shows. It was a hobby."

Gus couldn't hold back anymore.

"Ma'am, I don't mean to pry, but I believe the tapes you gave me belong to your son. May I speak with him?"

The old woman frowned and tapped her wrinkled hand against the arm of her chair.

"Mr. Spectra, I hope you enjoy the gift I've given you and you can listen to the tapes all you like. But, I'm going to have to ask you to leave now."

She rose gracefully from her seat and walked toward the door. He complied and followed.

"Ma'am, I hope I didn't offend you. I do apologize. It's just the music on those tapes was brilliant. The best I've heard in thirty years, since Elvis—the Stones—the Beatles, and I think the rest of the world needs to hear your son, too."

The old woman became even angrier.

"Goodbye, Sir."

Gus nodded and walked down the front steps to his car. He heard the door slam hard behind him.

* * *

*

Over the next three months, Gus stopped going to yard sales. Instead, he became a bit of a private investigator, sitting in his Saab for hours across the street from the white Victorian. He would take a brown-bag lunch and sodas, and study the activities of the family. He learned their name was Landon, the mother, Bernice, and the father, George, both in their seventies, both devout Catholics, who attended church daily. George was a pipe smoker and Bernice, cigarettes. The old man spent hours on the lawn, desperately watering the yellow turf, hoping that some miracle could overcome the New England summer and relentless sun. But, it was too damaged; nothing would revive it. He followed Bernice as she went to lunch with friends at the country club twice a week and George as he listened to the Red Sox on his transistor radio while sitting in the side yard in his lawn chair. He drove behind George and his exercise routine: walking four miles a day with iron dumbbells. He wrote his observations in his old leather notebook.

Then, around July, Gus started knocking on the neighbors' doors, asking them questions about the Landons' son. He found quite quickly that the neighborhood was primarily Irish: Murphy, Flaherty, Molloy, Bradley, Ronan, O'Reilly, Fitzpatrick, and except among themselves, they refused to share personal information, especially to a complete stranger. No one seemed to know anything about the Landon boy when Gus asked. He suspected that Mrs. Landon had gotten to them, told them that some yard sale vagrant had forced his way into their house and asked inappropriate questions about the recorder and their boy. "Can't trust strangers these days," she must've said. "Being kind will just get you in trouble."

By August, Gus had an address. He met a couple of high school kids outside the local Dunkin' Donuts and asked them if they knew about the Landon boy. One teenager in a blue Liverpool soccer jersey finally caved when Gus offered to buy him some cigarettes. The kid gave Gus the info and asked him not to tell anyone that he'd talked to him. Gus agreed wholeheartedly. Doctor-patient confidentiality was still deep inside him.

Gus knew where he was going the whole time he drove down Route 1 and finally realized the nature of the boy's illness. He knew now that the Landon boy was not in good shape. His Saab pulled up in front of the hospital and he looked at the sign on the black iron gates: *Charles Berry Memorial Hospital.*

Gilda had been his secretary for fifteen years and in many ways was like his second wife. They'd never had an affair, but spent late nights talking to each other. She had helped him through a lot and whenever Dusty needed a mother figure, Gilda was certainly there for him.

He walked through the halls of the old hospital, studying the marble floor and the murals of old New England hanging on the walls. He came upon his old office and walked in hesitantly.

Gilda sat at a computer typing and when she looked up to see him, an astonished look came upon her face.

"Oh my God. Dr. Spectra—Gus. How are you?" she blurted out.

"Fine, Gilda. You?"

She rose from her chair and hugged him. Tears came to her eyes and he rubbed her back gently to comfort her.

"I'm so sorry," she whispered. "There was nothing I could do or say."

Gus pushed her back and smiled. He nodded to her desk that was covered with paperwork and folders of the patients.

"I need a favor."

*

Gus walked slowly onto the green lawn of the hospital and studied a group of patients having their afternoon free time. He didn't recognize many of them because they had not been there when he was a doctor. He prided himself on the fact that ninety-percent of the kids he worked with were back in society, functioning well, had jobs, returned to college or high school. He had healed them or at least helped them transition back into society.

● ● ●

141

Gilda was next to him and pointed across the lawn.

"There," she said. "He's the one in the lawn chair. The one with the guitar and leather jacket on."

Gus turned back to her, astonished, looking to see if she noticed his shock.

"I'm sorry, which one?"

"Right there, near the strawberry plants and arboretum," she said matter-of-factly. "But don't talk to him long, Gus. His parents have left strict instructions for no visitors. And, I don't know how the administration would feel about things, especially since—"

"Since what?" Gus prodded.

"Since he's in the suicide unit," she said, as gently as possible.

Gus looked out at the figure and felt the strange sensation run through his body.

He looked back at her. "Remember when I was good?"

Gilda smiled. "You still are, Gus. Just don't get me fired."

He hugged her and began walking slowly over the green lawn toward the figure in the lawn chair.

● ● ●

BEEN A SON

I spot his black BMW convertible pulling into the parking lot of the Coffee Bean on Wilshire. I'm sitting at a table, thinking about earthquakes and divine intervention, my two best options for disappearing right now. I feel my heart begin to sink into my stomach and try to straighten myself out—I don't want to give him the impression right away that anything is wrong. I'm not ready for this moment of revelation—this ignominy—that will affect both of our lives. It's a Friday morning in June. I'm back in Santa Monica from college, and I'm going to lunch with my father.

I think about Boston and how I'd give anything to be living there this summer, to make this all go away. I want to be shopping on Newbury, attending Red Sox games, taking the Red Line out to Cambridge for shows at the Middle East—getting drunk.

Instead, I'm back in California, alone in our family's condo in Santa Monica, left to contemplate the perfidy that I've committed, a responsibility that will change everything, including when and if I'll graduate from college.

* * *

I find it terribly ironic that I'm back in the land of bikinis and jeweled navel rings; I won't be wearing either this summer.

I stand up, and think to myself that this moment of revelation should really be a delicate one. It requires a more appropriate setting, not some coffee shop filled with a bunch of middle-aged, balding, pathetic screenwriters pounding out dialogue on their laptops while they Tweet their statuses, peruse Facebook, and e-mail their parents for money to keep the dream alive. This conversation deserves a more distinguished backdrop to ease his anger and pain. Unlike the rest of L.A., my problem is real, not celluloid.

I wonder if I should walk out, take my father's hand, lead him around the corner to St. Monica's and position ourselves in a confessional, so I can whisper my disgrace in his ear through a veiled screen like I did to the priest as a little girl for my first penance. That's what I was taught, right? Don't be afraid to tell my parents the truth. However, there will be no white lace dresses, envelopes of money, or reception at the Riviera Country Club this time around.

As I stand up, I realize my father will sense deception from miles away, like one of those seismographs reading earthquakes in the desert somewhere near the San Andreas Fault. As soon as he sees my face, he'll know; he's a businessman who deals with millions of dollars a day. He looks foreign men in the eye to see if they're lying. But it's more than that—it's our lifelong connection, one that goes back to when I was a little girl. It was like he knew this day would come, that he could only protect me for so long because of what I was: his daughter. Maybe his intuition came from his experience in the business world, or something he observed when we moved from Boston to Los Angeles. Maybe he just saw the way women were treated out here. I believe that a father knows his daughter better than anyone in the world. Mine is no different.

I stare back out at my dad, who is now waving at me through the window, from inside his black BMW—he's older, much grayer than I recall at Christmas, but still tan and healthy-looking, the quintessential Californian, a rich and sunbathed man with a strong jaw, Ray-Bans, and that futile surfer-turned-businessman look.

I try to shake off the surge of anxiety—that innate Catholic guilt that was embedded on my forehead at baptism. But, I suddenly notice my beige skirt has a stain on it and panicked, I grab a napkin to wipe if off, but it's too late—it has soaked in. Not even holy water can remove this stain.

I look back up at my own reflection in the glass. I'm not seven anymore—no longer daddy's little girl. Instead, I see myself: twenty-one years old, looking wan and fat. I pick up my purse to cover the stain, throw my empty cup of coffee away, then hesitantly push the door open. The sunlight shines down on me as I walk out, and it feels good for the first time since I've gotten off the plane. It's unseasonably hot—not gloomy as June is said to be. I open the car door and sit down on the hot leather seat.

"Hi Honey," says my father, leaning over to kiss me on the cheek. "Sorry—had a call from Tokyo."

I nod understandingly. In junior high, it was London; in high school, it was Dubai; he's moved farther east as I've gotten older. I catch a whiff of his aftershave—it's a scent of childhood, as memorable as our mid-winter trips to Palm Springs or Christmas morning in the living room of our old condo in Santa Monica before we moved to Sherman Oaks. He puts the car in gear and we zoom out to Wilshire, moving west toward the ocean. My hair blows back and I feel exhilarated by the sudden movement. An older, attractive blonde woman in a shiny white Mercedes pulls up next to us, smiling seductively at my dad, who in return nods chivalrously and speeds on.

"How's everything with you, Babe?" he asks, checking the rearview for the blonde. "Boston good?"

I wonder for a moment if he's dating anyone, or if he's stuck to his self-proclaimed Catholic beliefs: he'd often say, "I'm only getting married once." He keeps a penthouse in Century City and I'm sure there are women around. But I also know that my father is a man of his word. Maybe that's why I got fooled; I thought all men were honest.

"Fine. Boston's just fine," I reply. "Where are we going for lunch?"

"Bel Air Bay," he says. "I'm not dealing with traffic in Beverly Hills today. Let's stay on the West Side."

I'm fine with that; it's where I grew up and went to school. I think about who may be there, worrying that we might make a scene in front of my former classmates from Marymount or even worse, Corpus, my elementary school. My father is absolutely paranoid about exposing family matters to the public, especially when business associates or neighbors are around.

We sit at the stoplight at the intersection of Wilshire and Ocean for a moment, and I stare at the ivory statue of St. Monica. She is stoic, reverent, unmoving, her hands extended as if to say, "I'm ready, Lord. Whatever you've got." I wonder if the real woman was truly as strong as this concrete depiction of her.

The light changes to green and a gentle breeze blows my hair back again. I want to cut it, liberate myself during the sweltering summer that lurks ahead. It will certainly be a different experience being back in L.A. under this pretense I feel a nervous twinge in my stomach and wonder if I'll be sick in my father's new BMW.

He turns on the radio and Bono sings out, "With or Without You." My dad smiles reflectively.

"What?" I say, amused with his old-age quirkiness.

"You know, I always thought this would be a great wedding song," he says, humming along. I look at him weakly and force a smile back.

"It'll be *your* wedding day sometime soon," he continues with a sigh. "We'll probably be able to get St. Monica's and then we can all walk over to the Fairmount for the reception. How's that sound?"

I look away and catch a glimpse of a homeless woman pushing her shopping cart full of plastic bottles.

"Sounds wonderful," I respond.

"What's wrong?" asks my father. "You seem distant."

"Just worried about another earthquake," I joke.

"Wow, you remember that?"

"I was seven, Dad."

"Oh," he says with a frown. "I thought you were younger."

I look down at the ivory beach, lurking below the clear blue skies as we descend on the PCH. Catalina rises up in the distance and I wonder why I've never visited the island, even though it's just miles off the coastline. Memories of childhood flood my mind: long summer days at the beach club with my classmates from Catholic school. I wonder where those kids are now. I can't think of one whom I've been in touch with since I left Los Angeles for college in Boston.

"You know, even though I love Sherman Oaks," he says reminiscently, "I miss the old condo in Santa Monica. You were only five or six when we lived there. I kept it as an investment."

"I remember," I insist, finding the investment comment funny. He hadn't rented it for years.

"That was before we had money," he finishes. "And before you mother—"

"Dad," I interject a bit angrily. He becomes silent.

After a moment, the DJ comes on and announces that Morrissey will be playing the Hollywood Bowl. Then, "I'm So Sorry" emanates from the speakers and we move forward.

*

My father and I are sitting at a table by the window at the beach club and I'm watching shirtless teenage boys with tan torsos run toward the ocean with surfboards. I imagine it as a Beach Boys' video—the timeless shore and, if you told someone it was 1960 here, they'd have no problem believing you. I think about the bay and how they use to worry it was polluted a few years ago. Now, with the community's effort and the help of an environmental agency, it's allegedly safe. Purified. The bay was given a second chance, it seems.

"So, what's the plan for the summer? Did you send a resume to Citigroup like I suggested at Christmas?" my father asks, sipping from a glass of white wine. It's his second of the meal and I think it odd that he's going back to work on a multi-million-dollar deal later this afternoon.

"Yeah. They filled all their internships," I reply, without much in my voice.

"I can make a call," my dad offers.

"Why don't we wait and see?"

"Well, we're still members here, you know," he says reassuringly. "I've kept our dues up. You're welcome to ride your bike down and spend the day. I bring clients here once in a while, so no drinking."

"You don't have to worry about that."

I sip my Diet Coke. I notice the ice cubes are melting quickly, and suddenly feel flushed.

"And how's your mother?" he asks, looking away from me.

"I don't really know. I haven't seen her very much since I got in. We're having lunch tomorrow."

He nods and sips his wine.

"Well, she's certainly an enigma," he begins in a tone. "I speak to her on holidays, or to talk about your tuition or her bills. That's it."

"Dad…"

"Well, well—only one year of college to go," he says with a smile, promptly changing the subject. "My, my, my. What do you think of that? My little girl is growing up. Law or business school after that? I have some connections at USC, you know."

My stomach does a somersault. I shift in my seat and clear my throat. I despise his traditional-sounding tone and feel myself gag. A waiter comes over, smiles, fills our water glasses, and speaks to my dad, who replies in Spanish.

"I'm not sure what I'm going to do. Kind of living in the present," I continue.

"Your grades are okay, right? No surprises," he says with a concerned look.

"My grades are fine, Dad."

"Because if Boston isn't working out," he begins, "We're not from there anymore. I can easily get you transferred to USC for your senior year."

"No, no," I insist.

It's my situation that's the problem. A problem that I wish my business-minded father had a strategic solution for; a problem that stands in the way of my future.

* * *

"I took a class on Joyce this semester," I finally say.

"That's great," my father replies patronizingly. "But you're still a business major, I hope."

"I actually worked it out so I could minor in English," I tell him.

"Hey, I never signed anything on that," he replies jokingly. "Must've been your mother."

"Why don't you let up on her, Dad?" I say defensively. I know my mother is suffering in her own depression due to the collapse of her twenty-year marriage. A woman becoming single at forty-five is a challenge in Southern California.

"I'm sorry," he says, shaking his head. "I don't want to ruin lunch. It's just that I don't understand her sometimes."

"Well," I offer. "Neither do I."

I excuse myself to go to the bathroom and make it into a stall just before I throw up the contents of my stomach. I feel a cold sweat coming on and wonder if I should call my doctor back in Boston. I collect myself, wash my face, and stare into the mirror. I look pale and older, dark circles under my eyes. I wonder if I'm iron deficient, or maybe need more protein in my diet. I wait until the dizziness fades, then wipe my hands with a cloth towel and throw it in the hamper.

When I come back out, my father is eating his sandwich and my stomach aches when I see my waiting hamburger and fries. I sit back down and try to pretend that I wasn't vomiting thirty seconds before, trying to get my mind on more positive things.

"Everything okay?" he says to me with suspicious eyes. "You aren't doing drugs, are you, Honey?"

Silence.

"Dad," I finally say, looking away from him. "I'm pregnant."

I hear his fork hit his plate, and look up shamefully. He wipes his mouth with the embroidered napkin and looks across the table at me, pointing his finger in my face.

"That's it," he says angrily. "You're done. Finished."

He stands up, throws his napkin, along with some money, on the table, then storms out of the club in disgust. I sit for a moment, unemotional, and watch some kids building sand castles in the middle of the volleyball court.

*

The second most traumatic day of my life was the day of the San Bernardino earthquake of 1994; I was seven years old. It was a few weeks after Christmas and, as I walked home from school alone underneath the warmth of the January sun, I remember feeling pretty good about myself. My pathetic friends were back in Massachusetts playing in the stinging cold of an asphalt playground, while I got to come home to a swimming pool in my California backyard every afternoon. I thought I was cool—like a child star.

I remember walking home through the wind; it was strange: a warm backward zephyr blowing against my face, as if a storm was coming. I recall feeling different, but figured it was all part of coming to this new and exotic land called California.

Our two-bedroom house was located on a quiet, palm-tree-lined cul-de-sac overlooking The Valley; my parents had one bedroom, and I had the other. We had left the small condo in Santa Monica behind us—along with the noise, the smell, and the feeling that moving to California was a mistake. My dad had gotten a promotion and this home was the result his bonus.

"The condo is an investment," he told my mom. "Plus, I can stay there to get away from your nagging."

Sometimes, as I got older, I would sneak up on our roof, look down on Ventura Boulevard, and listen to "Free Fallin'" on my Walkman. Sometimes, I wondered if there were really vampires wandering through The Valley, or maybe zombies like in Michael Jackson's "Thriller" video.

But that day in 1994, I made my way up our brick driveway and went inside to find a snack waiting for me on the kitchen table. I heard my mom talking on the phone in the other room, and shouted that I was home. She came in a few minutes later and informed me that she didn't feel like cooking after her tennis lesson and garden club meeting, so we were going to pick up Kentucky Fried Chicken per the request of my father. I remember telling her about my day, then walking through our garage for the new purple bike from my grandmother, and riding around our cul-de-sac.

I remember feeling odd and alone in my driveway that day; I didn't have any new friends yet. I was alone frequently, left to my thoughts and imagination. The street was abnormally quiet in my new neighborhood, and the rubbery trunks of the palm trees bent as they swayed in the wind like fans at a concert. I remember odd things from that day, too, like the black Chevy truck with tinted windows that kept driving past me. Something about it made me feel creepy. I imagined being kidnapped like a local kid had been. He'd been taken down to Mexico, held for ransom. Drugs were involved. They found his body in Tijuana—his head and limbs cut off. But, the black truck moved on and finally my mother called me to wash up. The kidnappers had spared me.

That night, my father came home in a terrible mood—irritable and cranky. I remember him loosening his tie, looking hot and sweaty, his sleeves rolled up on his dress shirt as he drank two beers with dinner—the greasy buckets of Kentucky Fried Chicken that we had picked up in Studio City just past DuPar's on Ventura. He complained about everything—his new boss, the traffic on the 405 on his ride home from Century City, being away from our family back in Boston.

"Well then, take the canyon," my mother interjected.

"I'm not taking the goddamned canyon," he screamed at her. "It's slower."

"Well, I like it. It's a scenic ride," she replied, lighting another cigarette.

He seemed to need the alcohol to keep him sane. My mom chose nicotine as she politely endured his diatribe. I sat quietly, gnawing on my greasy drumstick, as my dad found another beer in the fridge.

After dinner, I put on my pajamas, did my homework, then watched *90210*, although my Mom sat warily and made sure no inappropriate content came on. I kind of related to the Walsh family and their recent move from Minnesota to Beverly Hills. My father paced the house restlessly, probably worried about his job, the economy, or maybe the new mortgage we had on this two-bedroom house in Sherman Oaks.

I finally went to bed around nine. I remember watching him through my bedroom window by our pool smoking my mother's cigarettes. I swear he sensed something. He just knew that something in nature wasn't right.

I woke in the early morning darkness to a rumbling. I sat up in bed and felt my heart pound inside my chest. Was this the end? Was I being punished by God for feeling good about my new pool and weekend trips to Disneyland? For twenty long seconds, our house shook as if it was being swallowed by the earth. Before I knew what was happening, my father sprinted into my room and grabbed me out of bed just as my huge bookshelf collapsed onto my mattress. Had he not been there, I would've been crushed to death. He held me in his strong arms and carried me out to the street. My father saved my life. To this day, only he and I know that.

*

When I was twelve, my father decided he wanted to turn me into Fred Lynn. I had grown tall, and was fast. I kept my hair short and wore a Boston Red Sox hat so, in many ways, I looked like a boy. I liked the attention he paid me, and on Saturdays he'd hit pop flies to me at the local ball field off of Ventura. I enjoyed our time together and the hamburgers and milkshakes that followed afterwards at In and Out Burger; it was our special time together, since he was always working so much.

However, one day he said something that bothered me. He'd hit me a pop fly with his Fungo bat and I slid hard into the earth of centerfield, making a fantastic catch.

"My God—you should've been a boy," he said, shaking his head. "Should've been my son, not my daughter, with athletic ability like that."

I was confused. Did he not want a daughter, or was he embarrassed of me as a person? Did he want a boy who could've been a varsity baseball player, maybe make it to the majors some day and play for the Red Sox? All my friends were Dodgers' fans and I was secretly starting to like them, too.

During childhood, he was obsessed with telling me about Fred Lynn.

"Best goddamned center fielder the Sox ever had. MVP and Rookie of the Year in 1975," said my dad to the image of an aging man with a mustache as he stood at bat in his San Diego Padres uniform. "Can't believe they gave him away to the Angels, but he wanted to come home to California. Too many injuries."

"Maybe he liked it better out here," I replied.

"Like it here? He was from here: USC! You see, California ball players are the best. It's the goddamned weather," he'd proclaim to me as I played with my Barbie dolls. "DiMaggio, Williams, they were born in San Francisco and San Diego!"

I didn't make the connection at such a young age between hitting a baseball and warm weather. I contemplated his words and exhaled.

"Are you sad that I was a girl?" I finally asked.

"No, no Honey," he said with a smile, ruffling my hair. "Just keep your head on straight," he told me. "You have an opportunity, Sweetheart. You're a pretty girl who is so smart. Do something with your life. Just don't let some boy go and screw it up."

*

I am walking down Montana Avenue, past a high-class clothing boutique, and I see, through the large glass window, my mother sitting at a small table in Café Montana. She doesn't notice me for a moment and I study her aging face, purple dress, and white pearls around her neck. She looks older than my father, and I wonder if it's stress or the pack of cigarettes I know she still smokes every day. I feel my stomach churn with anxiety. She suddenly turns and, with a surprised expression on her face, sees me, then waves for me to come in.

After a hug and kiss, I sit down with her and notice that she has ordered a glass of red wine for herself. The waitress comes over and asks me what I want.

"Just water, please," I respond, recalling my experience with Diet Coke the day before.

My mother reaches across the table and grabs my hands.

"How are you feeling?" she asks in a concerned voice.

"Fine, Mom," I reassure her.

"Have you made a decision about school?" she asks.

"No. Not yet," I respond. "I'll probably go back, I mean, I'm not sure. We'll see."

"Have you told the boy?"

"Mom," I say. "It's complicated."

"We'll, whoever he is, he has to realize his responsibility. Men never take responsibility. Your father, for example," she stammers, taking a big sip of wine.

"It's my responsibility, too," I remind her.

"Well, that's convenient for you to say," she says with a huff. "You're not the one paying for it."

I smile, but the idea of money scares me and I study the menu. I go with a chicken entrée salad; she orders a steak.

"So, did you tell me, or your father, first?" she asks, rubbing her chin nervously.

"Does it matter, Mom?"

"He always knew you inside and out," she says. "I always had to pry these things out of you. You always hid things from me. "

"Mom, I tell you everything."

"Apparently not," she says. "Fortunately, we don't go up to Corpus Christi anymore. This would be quite the little scandal for them. Those women up there would love to sink their teeth into this gossip."

I nod and think about some of the more serious scandals the church has dealt with. A college girl getting pregnant would be the least of their worries. Dinner comes and we eat silently, watching the foot traffic on Montana: skinny pregnant mothers going to yoga or for a pedicure; joggers moving toward the beach; that homeless woman pushing a shopping cart with the plastic bottles.

"Keanu Reeves was in here last week," my mother finally says. "He's dating that girl from the vampire film. It was in *People*."

I nod and long for the anonymous winter streets of Boston, staggering around in the cold as I walked home from class. There's something about being outside and needing to seek warmth. When you live in California, you take the good weather for granted. The only reminder is during February when it rains and rains for days. June can be cloudy, but I haven't seen the sun go away since I've been back.

"So, the condo..." my mother begins. "Did your father tell you?"

"No. What?" I ask, my voice alarmed. It's the haven that protects me from being interrogated by my parents.

"Well, that's typical of him."

"Why? What about the condo?" I demand.

"We're selling it," she says. "Something in the divorce settlement. We must keep everything equal—fifty-fifty in California, you know."

"Well, where will I live?" I ask in a frightened tone. The condo is part of my plan; I need it. If I am going to stay in Santa Monica, I figure I can raise my baby there.

"You'll have to move back to Sherman Oaks. Back to your old room," says my mom, pointing to her empty wine glass as the waitress comes by. The waitress takes it to the bar quickly to get it refilled.

"No, Mom," I insist. "That's not going to work. I planned on—"

"We all make plans in life, Darling," she says sharply, with a swig from her new glass.

"But I need space, and I have no money."

"Well, then, go back to Boston," she says, accepting her new glass of wine from the waitress. "See if I care."

I look at her bitter face and realize that I never disliked my mom; I just never related to her.

*

It's the Fourth of July and I'm at a cookout in the Palisades. A friend of mine from Corpus convinced me to come up for the parade. She's talking with Luke Wilson, who is apparently a neighbor. A handsome blonde guy, who informs me he went to Loyola then Stanford business school, talks to me in slurred speech. I'm still not showing and my blouse would hide anyway, so he has no clue. His breath smells like keg beer and I feel embarrassed for him, even though he makes $350,000 a year and tells me that he just bought a lot that overlooks the Bel Air Bay Club.

"Do you want to come and watch the fireworks with us tonight?" he asks, sounding like a stroke victim.

I smile at him and excuse myself for the bathroom, then leave.

*

When I was at college in Boston, I was part of a group: a pro-life group. I didn't intend to get involved, but my boyfriend kind of coaxed me into it. Things happen that way at academically progressive colleges. And truthfully, it was all part of the delirium—I was infatuated with him. He was the first boy I had ever really been with. He was the first one I loved, the first one I trusted.

Between our classes, there were meetings, rallies, marches, passionate speeches by student leaders and Jesuits who were devoted to the cause. I spent much of my free time with the group and this boy. We got close. One thing led to another one night and before I knew what had happened, I was pregnant.

The boy apparently wasn't as attached to the pro-life movement as he claimed because he left it as quickly as he left me. Just after Easter, he informed me he was spending his junior year abroad in Ireland.

"I guess I need to reexamine my own conscience," he told me just before the year ended. "And I think you should get rid of the baby. We have our futures in front of us, and I don't think I can do this. I'm sorry."

He turned and walked away from me. I stood in the campus quad and watched his shadow disappear into the darkness. For a moment, I actually wished that I could be a boy—so I could walk away, too.

It's late September and I feel strange not going back to school. It's an unseasonably warm day in Santa Monica and a moving truck arrives at my apartment early. Hispanic men come in and start taking boxes out. I offer them cold bottled water but they shake their heads "no" and keep working. I don't have much—my possessions have been sent for in Boston, but the condo apparently has been sold and all the furniture must go as well.

My father's BMW pulls up around noon. He's wearing a light, tailored Italian suit. I haven't seen him since the day at the club and he offers no words to me but barks commands at the Hispanic men. He puts his hands on his hips, inspects the work, but doesn't make eye contact with me. After a few minutes, he puts his Ray-Bans back on, gets in his BMW, then speeds off down Wilshire.

*

I'm sitting on the roof of my childhood house in Sherman Oaks. I hear someone coming up the creaky ladder behind me, but don't turn around. My father sits down and stares out toward The Valley. The traffic is backed up on Ventura again.

"I'm sorry about today," he says finally. "Actually, I'm sorry about everything."

"Dad…"

"No, let me talk," he blurts firmly. "I've acted like an animal. You are my daughter and I need to protect you."

"You already have, Dad. I'm the one who screwed up."

"I have a confession to make," he says, after a moment of silence.

I turn and look at him a bit stunned. I don't think my father has ever opened up to me in this way. It's like the priest confessing to the communicant. I feel nervous. He digs his Italian shoes into the curved red Romanesque tiles. There's one that was chipped in the earthquake and cracked from the sun still hanging on to the slant. With his heel, he sends the piece over the edge into our driveway. I hear it shatter below.

"The condo in Santa Monica—you know how I always said we kept it as an investment?"

"Yeah," I reply, suddenly feeling the baby kick hard. I am six months along.

"Well, the truth is—it was for a woman," he pauses, ashamed. "A woman with whom I was having an affair for many years."

My heart sinks. I think back to the '90s. There had been a tenant there—a woman with a young baby. I'd gone and played with the boy a few times when my father had stopped by to pick up the rent check. I looked at him incredulously.

"We had a child together," he continues. "It was complicated, Honey. Your mother couldn't have any more children and…"

"And you wanted a son," I whisper.

"Yes," he confesses. "I wanted a son."

I nod and hear him sniffle. I wonder if they are crocodile tears, too little, too late. I feel the kicking again and weigh my options. I want to escape. I want to leave with my baby, move into a cabin up in some vineyard of Santa Barbara, or maybe go south, far away to Mexico, where maybe, just maybe, that little boy who was kidnapped when I was a younger wasn't killed. Maybe he's down there alive, now grown up, raised by a nice Mexican family.

I think about jumping off this roof and going back to Boston. I think about finishing my senior year with my baby strapped to my chest in a Bjorn, walking to class as the other girls stare at me disdainfully. I think about how I wish the earthquake had swallowed me up like the others who had died fifteen years ago.

I think about how I never really knew my father at all. And, I think about how I should've been a son.

* * *

BAPTISM

I arrive home from my audition for *Last Comic Standing* holding a grocery bag containing two bottles of cheap merlot and an ounce of weed, when I notice a conspicuous FedEx envelope hanging out of my crooked mailbox that overlooks Wilshire. I hesitate for a moment, then slowly set down the bag and take a giant step back. I dig into my jeans pocket and produce a cigarette, light it, then blow a cloud of smoke at my rusty mailbox as if I am engaged in an ancient ritual that will lure the demons from this overnight express package. I wonder if the weed might be more effective.

Right now, nothing seems to consume me more than this envelope. Not the fact that I've sat in traffic for the last two hours on the 10 Freeway on my way back from Hollywood, or the stinging words of a short, bald, gay producer: "Yeah—we'll let you know." Not even the fact that I'm broke and unemployed, or that, despite the temperate California sun, I'm homesick and a little depressed.

For some reason, I recall Palm Sunday Mass in 1981 when, as an awkward eleven-year-old altar boy, I ignited the incense in a gold-chained urn for the priest to disperse upon the congregation. As the smoke rose up into my nose, the pungent frankincense billowing from the urn overtook me.

• • •

And, as I followed the priest up and down the aisles, I felt that same sick feeling that's in my gut right now. Upon returning to the altar, I promptly puked into the baptismal pool. My Irish-Catholic mother has never forgiven me, and to this day I spurn the smell of frankincense.

What the hell is it? I wonder, released from my disturbing memory. *A warrant for my arrest for unpaid parking tickets? Maybe a collections notice for that credit card?*

However, my gut tells me it's something far worse, something that's going to change my life. Something so horrendous I may have no other choice but go back up to Malibu for another thirty days and spend my afternoons with the resident psychologist as I lie in a lawn chair that overlooks the Pacific, telling him how Hollywood has fucked me up and how I've let my Irish-Catholic family down with my reckless behavior, loss of morals, and general disregard for my own well-being.

I feel a mounting in my chest, an apprehension, an instinctive need for survival that originates in the diaphragm and creates a fear so real that you either fight or flee. It is one only familiar if you have suffered a tragedy, or if you consume the amount of caffeine and nicotine I do.

But maybe, it occurs to me, this package is something good, like an acceptance letter for a comedic screenplay that I sent out months ago or a forgotten residual check. I finally reach for the FedEx envelope and rip it open.

Inside, I find a note that reads: *Come back to Boston and be godfather to your nephew. Be for little James what Uncle James was for us. We forgive you. Love—your sister—Mary.*

Attached to the note are a round-trip plane ticket and a check for any "incidentals." I stare at both for a few minutes and then go inside my rent-controlled $800-a-month shit-hole apartment. I uncork the merlot and drink it from a green plastic Celtics tumbler. I go back outside and smoke two more cigarettes on my stoop, then promptly take the check down to the Bank of Santa Monica and cash it. There, I try making eyes at the blonde bank teller, as if I have transformed into Leo DiCaprio in *Catch Me If You Can*. I feel slightly paranoid as she counts out the five hundred dollars in twenties, then smiles and sets them in my palm. As I slide the greenbacks into a bank envelope, it suddenly occurs to me that my "incidentals" probably differ from my sister's.

■ ■ ■

I make my way back up Wilshire, stop at 11th Street Liquors and buy a pack of Camels, then head directly to Sonny's to get drunk.

"Godfather? Who wants to be a godfather?" I ask myself aloud as I pass a homeless woman sleeping in a doorway in the iridescent sunlight, covered with a dirty blanket. I notice that, oddly, underneath her head are wilted palm leaves. For me, this should be just another typical drunk afternoon in Santa Monica, but as I walk beneath the warm sunshine something feels different; something has changed inside me. I feel like Lazarus raised from the dead.

Nine months have passed since I drove my parents to my Uncle James's funeral in Connecticut. My sister is always pregnant at funerals. My nephew, James, was born shortly afterward, her first son after four failed attempts. In the Catholic Church, there is no mandatory time frame for a baptism; it's simply decided by the parents and usually held within a reasonable period from the child's birth. As I finish my first beer, I realize my sister has been waiting for me.

She also probably knows that I've squandered all the envelopes of money and inheritance that my dead uncle sent me. For two months after his funeral and my return to L.A., there was nothing—I was broke and wondering if my days were numbered on the West Coast. I started surfing Craigslist, looking for part-time jobs, anything to keep me here; it seemed over. But then, miraculously, I'd experienced an unusual streak of luck.

In January, I landed a Capital One commercial and five speaking lines in a scene with Spalding James on *Legal Las Vegas*. I'd walked away with forty grand in residuals when all was said and done. Then, I paid my rent for a year, as well as some lingering credit card debt, bought a used Volvo, and drank the rest away at Sonny's and various ritzy bars on the Sunset Strip. Never mind Vegas. I never told anyone back home about the actual amount of money I'd made; I stopped bragging about almost-successes a long time ago.

Things happen this way in L.A.; it's as if you're in some kind of a time continuum and what occurs in the West doesn't always have viability in the East.

I landed an agent named Mel Berman, who kept an office off Ventura Boulevard in Studio City and took $10,000 of my earnings before I'd even seen my first check. Then, after I showed up drunk for a couple of auditions, Mel just stopped calling. For a while, things seemed to be happening for me; then as usual, my luck changed.

As I sit at the bar in Sonny's and sip my second Stella I realize I haven't eaten all day, so I order some Chinese barbecue buffalo fingers and study the crowd. Everyone in the place is trying to "make it" in Hollywood one way or another. It's like Rick's in *Casablanca*: a bunch of people waiting for their letters of transit, only to Hollywood success. Then, they come back here to wallow in their failure or, occasionally, to celebrate with a glimmer of hope in their eyes. It comes in different forms: a job as a P.A. or an extra; one guy gets a Nicorette commercial, another a national Target spot. Some get excited if they land a call back or like my friend, J.V., even score a reality show and a slot on *Deal or No Deal*, where he wins a hundred and eighty grand. Hollywood gives you just enough hope if you're one of us; just enough to keep you here for another year.

I recall the night they first ran the bank commercial on national television during a Patriots playoff game. I was the one who bought rounds for everyone and fed the jukebox dollar bills until closing. I had been a "local" hero of sorts, rubbing elbows with a bunch of drunken expatriates from Boston. But when my money dwindled, so did the friendships. When you fail in L.A., no one wants to be near you: you're bad luck.

I think of my old friend Israel Schwartzman and wonder where he is right now, because I could use his advice. We'd come out from the East together; he'd made it immediately, while I'd struggled doing open mics and working part-time jobs. However, despite his success and my failure, our friendship remained alive. In fact, he'd set me up with Mary, a pretty Catholic girl from Studio City through his fiancée, Dea, but that had fallen apart when she realized I was more interested in drinking with my friends and rubbing elbows with people with connections than going out for quiet dinners or to artsy movies at the Arclight Cinemas in Hollywood.

I'd changed. It was something that I felt every day; conversations with people that dwindled when I realized they weren't going to help my career. Schwartzman had scored a gig as an assistant director on a reality show being shot on location in New Zealand called *Checkered Fools*, about

* * *

166

American waiters trying to make it at a five-star restaurant in Auckland. So for the winter, I had been on my own. And when the rains of February come in L.A., alone is not a good place to be.

The bartender, Jason, comes over and sets down another Stella. My third or fourth; I'm already losing track. He grew up south of Boston in Hull, a few towns over from mine, so I tell him about the news I've received from my sister.

"Flying back tomorrow," I say casually.

"Why?" he inquires. "It's cold."

"Gonna be a godfather," I laugh, sipping my beer.

"Hey! Just like the movie," he jokes.

"Yeah," I reply softly. "Just like the movie."

"That's an East Coast thing, still," he says with a serious tone as he leans forward on the bar. "Most people don't get to those rituals out here, do they?"

"No," I say. "They don't." And I drink.

*

Last July, I got a bad sunburn one Saturday afternoon. Mary, the girl from Studio City whom Dea had set me up with, enjoyed watching the jets land by LAX, on Dockweiler Beach in Playa del Rey. My pale skin doesn't respond well to the California sun, or any other warm-weather location. I remember as child I had a bad burn one summer in Florida and for many years, I shunned the sun. But this girl was blonde, beautiful, and *connected*: a nanny for a big agent at CAA up in the Palisades. In L.A., you're connected when you live in the same house and take care of the kids of a movie executive. I pretty much followed her lead on whatever she wanted to partake in, including sunbathing, sex, and the occasional five o'clock Mass at St. Monica's to make us feel better about all the sinning we were doing. I'd give her various comedy scripts to read, but she never passed any on because she said they weren't ready yet.

"Gabriel, you only get one shot with Hollywood," she'd insist. "You can't blow it with a script that isn't ready. They don't accept anything less than perfection."

I never knew if she was lying or even if she had read them. But finally, I got bored with her and her beach obsession and subsequently cheated on her with a barista from Starbucks who was an aspiring actress from Westwood and had scored a few speaking lines on *How I Met Your Mother*. I have no regrets because I'm pale and hate getting sunburned while watching jets land by that runway beach over by LAX. In the end, Schwartzman understood, but it took Dea a while to get over the break-up.

*

I am standing outside of Terminal B at Logan International and a yellow cab drives by me and splashes slush on my indigo-dyed jeans and black leather cowboy boots. It's the day before Easter, I'm hung over, and it's snowing heavily in Boston. I shake the slush off my leg and look around for my sister's silver Volvo X-90 SUV, but see only green Peter Pan buses and yellow cabs. A guy with long hair and a black guitar case is next to me and asks me for a match. I give him one and then light my own Camel. He smiles then nods to the gold coin in my hand that I've been nervously rotating between my fingers.

"When'd you get out, Dude?" he inquires.

"What?"

"Of rehab?" he questions. I stick the gold coin in my jeans pocket, pick up my suitcase, and walk abruptly away.

*

My sister shows up an hour later and I get in her Volvo, shivering, but don't question where she was. She apologizes anyway, and asks if I've been drinking because I smell like smoke and that usually goes with it. I assure her I'm sober, even though I had three drinks on the plane and have a flask of Jameson in my coat pocket.

"Good," she replies. "Because if you screw up this baptism, I'll never forgive you, Gabriel. And neither will Mom."

I ignore her and turn on the seat warmer as she steers, then digs through her Coach purse for the $3.50 toll to get into the Sumner Tunnel. She pays, shakes her head, then glances at me.

"You look skinny," she says. "They feed you at that place?"

We emerge from the darkness onto Storrow and I look out at the frozen river and the joggers who move steadily down the path next to the Charles as if they are unaware that it feels like winter. I recall running here in college, miles and miles, all the way from Newton and back. I breathe a sigh of relief that that chapter of my life is over; it all seemed a bit hopeless—running in circles.

We get off at the Copley exit a few minutes later and then drive up Beacon. The streets are scattered with students and tourists in town for the holiday, the marathon, and the Red Sox opener. As we pass through Kenmore, I wonder where the sun and cherry blossoms are and why I just left 70-degree temperatures. I start to think more fondly of that beach in Playa Del Rey.

A few minutes later, we get to my sister's brick colonial house in Brookline, a couple of blocks from the house where JFK was born, which is now a museum. I shake hands with my brother-in-law, who is shoveling the front stone walk. He leans on his shovel, and says how much he loved the Capital One commercial and my scene on *Legal Las Vegas*. I smile weakly, look at his house, and wonder what he's got in his liquor cabinet.

Inside, I take off my coat and feel the surge of heat from their brick fireplace. This is not my childhood home, but it feels good to be in a real house again. My four nieces run in and hug me as *Barney* plays on a plasma television in their playroom and mugs of hot chocolate steam on the Pottery Barn coffee table. My sister comes out of the kitchen with a silver tray and pours two cups of coffee from a stainless steel Krups carafe, handing me one. I assume that the maid must've brewed it before she was let off for the holiday. I walk into the other room and sit at the kitchen table, studying the paintings and drawings on the stainless steel fridge that my nieces have drawn at school and think of

* * *

my own art as a child, how good it felt when an adult acknowledged what I'd done. I watch my sister walk into the other room and strain to hear her remind my brother-in-law to hide all the booze and the prescription medicine just in case I have a relapse.

The Swedish nanny then appears holding the infant, my nephew James, and I smile at her. By the expression on her face and distance she keeps from me, she seems to already know my story. She asks if I'd like to hold my godson-to-be and I decline, letting my nieces fawn over him. She's not surprised. I've never held a baby in my life, and I respond the same way when asked if I wanted to hold my nieces when they were young. I look up at my sister, who is leaning against the alcove with her arms folded. She fingers her wedding ring nervously, and finally announces that she's going to start dinner.

I get comfortable on the living room couch and watch a preview of the Boston Marathon, then set down my cup of coffee and wonder when my parents are going to show up. My brother-in-law comes in and warms his hands by the fire, then smiles at me as if he's forgotten.

"Want a beer?"

"No, thanks," I say.

My sister walks in and looks at him angrily as his face turns scarlet.

"What did you just ask him?" she demands.

"It's okay," I stammer, and lie back on the couch.

"I'll go make up your bed," she says, storming out of the room.

"Sorry," apologizes my brother-in-law, shrugging his shoulders. "I forgot for a minute."

"It's not a big deal," I say, sitting back down. "I forget all the time."

I lean back into the soft red couch that cost more than my rent and feel the jet lag kick in a bit as the commentator talks about how it may snow again on Easter. I think to myself that it's good to be home, as my body fights the wave of fatigue brought on by the East.

*

I dream about drinking cold draft beer all day between Sonny's, the Lobster, and Big Dean's by the Santa Monica Pier, then riding my mountain bike until I hit Manhattan Beach, filled with flawless human beings running and jumping up and down in the clear sand. I feel good in the hot sun—intoxicated. I ride out to the end of the pier and come across a woman who looks like the Virgin Mary, holding a baby, looking at me strangely. Then, without warning, she turns and throws the infant into the Pacific. I jump in the surf to save the baby, but I can't find the child and feel sharks and eels brush against the bottom of my feet. I come to the surface and a fisherman shouts down from above that he's got the child, and reels in the baby. The taste of salt water is bitter in my mouth. The child has drowned.

*

I open my eyes to see my father staring down at me.

"Get up," he barks. "The goddamned coffee maker's broken. We need to buy a new one. Let's go."

I sit up, put my bare feet on the cold hardwood floor, and see that it's seven in the morning on Easter Sunday. I stagger out of bed and find my jeans draped over a chair with my suede jacket, and assume my sister put them there. I pull them on quickly, then stumble out into the hallway with my shoes in hand, and down the stairs to the front door. The new-used Grand Marquis sits in the driveway and my father beeps the horn. I instinctively take out a cigarette and light it, then walk toward the car, the smoke billowing in the cold. I open the door and start to get in. My father points at me.

"There's no smoking in this car," he yells. "Put it out. Get rid of it."

I toss the cigarette into the snow of the stone driveway, get in, and slam the door shut. I feel hung over, but know I didn't drink anything the night before and assume it's dehydration from flying or my little happy hour with a shot and some sleeping pills on the plane.

"It's Easter," I remind him. "Nothing's going to be open."

He shakes his head and pulls onto Beacon, driving past Coolidge Corner. I stare at the empty Green Line train as it passes us in the center of the road.

"Your sister thought Target might be. Things have changed around here," he says. "Starbucks everywhere. One right there and two more up the street."

He points to one on Beacon and shakes his head.

"I don't like it one bit," he says. "Corporate bullshit."

"There's nothing open," I repeat, as he steers over the MassPike then into Kenmore Square.

"Gabriel, when the Jews are involved, it doesn't matter. There's money to be made. Didn't that Berman fellow take something out of your paycheck for getting you that commercial?"

I say nothing. He must've heard from my sister.

My father shakes his head and we cross over to Commonwealth Avenue, then turn left onto the ramp to Storrow by Boston University.

"I think there's a Target up by Andrew Square," I finally say. "But it's not open."

"Roxbury?" he says. "Jesus. You think I'm taking this luxury automobile to Roxbury?"

I sink back into the seat and look out to my right at the Hancock and Prudential as we emerge from the darkness of the tunnel.

"You bring your dark suit? The fancy, three-button one?" he asks. "The one your Uncle James bought you?"

I didn't think he knew I'd used his dead brother's money for that. Probably my sister again.

"Yeah, I know about those envelopes," he says, shaking his head.

"The suit is pressed, in a garment bag back at your daughter's million-dollar house," I reassure him. "I wear it to a lot of auditions."

My father looks at me, betrayed.

"You better not," he mutters under his breath. "Godamned Hollywood."

Ten minutes later, we are sitting in the empty parking lot of Target and Home Depot. My father just shakes his head.

"Jesus Christ," he says, hitting the wheel in a fit.

"There's always Dunkin' Donuts," I offer.

"Is that your answer for everything?" he says. "Fast-food solution? Well, let me tell you something, Harry Hollywood, life doesn't work that way. And you're going to be dead like your damn aunt and cousin if you don't stop this crap right now."

We pull back into the city and pass through Kenmore. The car is silent and I recall our journey to Connecticut and how he had yelled at me like I was a child. I stare out at Fenway, half-pouting, and think of all the games I attended with my Uncle James when I was a kid.

"Where's Mom?" I ask.

"She's still sleeping," he says. "Going straight to the church."

*

I walk back into my sister's brick colonial holding a tray of Starbucks coffee for everyone, set it on the hallway table, and go upstairs to my room to get ready. I shower quickly and put on the Brooks Brothers suit, hoping that my sister will be impressed with my appearance. I hear my father shouting at my nieces to get ready and that we'll be late.

On the ride to the church, my dad looks over at me.

"You look good," he says, softly.

"Thanks," I say, feeling like a six-year-old again.

"I remember your baptism," he continues. "You cried like a baby."

"I was a baby," I laugh.

"Not your sister, though," he says. "She just smiled the whole time. You were always the whiner around here."

"Thanks," I reply. "I appreciate your selective memory."

"I think you'd better go to confession before you go up on that altar."

"Why?" I ask.

"Thirty days in a rehab program? You think I don't know about this stuff? I work with substance abuse counselors on a daily basis."

"You're a high school guidance counselor," I say disdainfully.

He slams on the brakes and I think for the first time since I was eight, when I accidentally elbowed my sister in the teeth, that he might smack me. I brace myself, but he pulls back his hand and shakes his head.

"God is watching you, Gabriel," he says, as he pulls into the church parking lot. "You can fool me, but you can't fool him."

*

Inside the church, everyone gathers around the altar. The baptism will take place before the eleven o'clock Easter Mass. My brother-in-law's uncle is the pastor of St. Loyola, a Jesuit from B.C. who pretty much calls all the shots and fits us in. The buzz in the crowd is that he may be considered for bishop soon; he has been in talks with Rome. I see my mother, dressed in a dark purple Talbots outfit, coming up the maroon rug of the center aisle. She sees me, comes over and hugs me.

"It's good that you've come home," she says softly in my ear. "How are you, Gabriel?"

"Good, Ma," I reply. "I'm better, really."

"Stand up straight up now. You look skinny," she says like Schwartzman's Jewish grandmother, whom I met only once, just before she died of a brain tumor at Cedar Sinai. My mother fixes the collar and lapel on my suit and frowns. "You wore the maroon tie? It looks sharp but it is Easter, Honey. Something purple would've been more appropriate."

It occurs to me that both Catholic and Jewish mothers are equally obsessed with posture and dress attire.

I can feel the anxiety rising in my chest, the same nervousness I felt before I walked out on the altar at my First Communion as a kid and looked down at her in the pew. The same nervousness I felt on Palm Sunday, 1981. I kiss her on the cheek and stand to the side, trying to breathe. My relatives are all over the church: my cousins from Rhode Island with my aunt and uncle who retired down in Newport. The Connecticut relatives wander around, too, mingling with my brother-in-law's large family from Brookline.

The baptism begins and I stand on the altar with my sister, brother-in-law, his sister from Wellesley, and the priest. My sister holds the baby tightly in her arms and looks at me with a smile, and then the priest, as he begins.

"What is the name you give to this child?"

"James Gabriel Flatley," my brother-in-law and sister say in unison, as if they have rehearsed it for the congregation.

"What do you ask of the church for this child?"

They respond and I look down at my hands to see that they are visibly shaking. I immediately jam them into my pockets.

"You have asked to have your child baptized," the priest continues. "And, in so doing, you are accepting the responsibility of training him in the practice of the faith. It will be your duty to bring him up to keep God's commandments as Christ taught us, by loving God and our neighbor. Parents, do you clearly understand what you are undertaking?"

"Yes," they reply together.

The baptism goes on and we are summoned to pay witness. I watch as the priest sprinkles holy water on James's tiny clavicle, and smile for a moment with a feeling inside that everything might be okay. He is the baptized, the "Catechumen," as I recall from my altar-boy days. The priest suddenly produces a small gold urn with chrism and crosses it on my nephew's head as he responds with a screaming cry. My sister pulls the baby back instinctively as the priest finishes, and looks over at me.

"Gabriel," she says. "Take him."

I look at my mother and my father, embarrassed. This probably means more to them than it does to my sister. Reluctantly, I take little James into my arms as the priest begins to speak about my responsibilities to my godson as I stand before God. I think I should feel something—but I don't, and feel awful about it. I tune out the priest and the only thing I can think about is getting this kid out of

• • •

my hands because I'm terrified I'm going to drop him to his death before he even sees his first Red Sox game and gets to tack posters of his heroes to his bedroom wall. I hand James back, and when the ceremony ends I exit the church through the back door without letting anyone know.

*

Around Boylston Street, I finally slow to a walk. I've easily made it a mile from the church, which is impressive since I haven't run in a while and smoke like a fiend. I am sweating and wipe the perspiration from my head, and lean against the wall outside the Pour House and think about going in and spending the cash I have left from the incidental check my sister sent me. Instead, I walk on past Copley and the Prudential to the Boston Public Library, and sit on the concrete steps for a moment. I take out a cigarette and light it, noticing that my hands have calmed themselves during my escape. They are huge, veiny, and red from the cold air.

I look at empty Copley Square, the Hancock Building, and the Plaza. It's barren for the most part, due to the cold weather, scattered piles of snow around, and the fact that it's Easter Sunday and all of the college students have gone home to be with their families, where I should be. I think about the post-baptismal reception that's going on at my sister's house back in Brookline and how people are sipping coffee and wine while chatting in soft voices. I am the prodigal son with nothing but a one-leg ticket back to LAX and no girlfriend to pick him up when he gets there. The joke, it seems, is on me.

*

I end up in a coffee house on Newbury Street, drinking mocha cappuccinos for an hour and staring at families arriving for Easter dinner at the Capitol Grill. A barista, who is probably a gay Emerson student, comes over to me and looks at my third empty cup.

"Sir," he says. "We're closing in five minutes. It *is* Easter."

"No problem," I respond, handing him my empty cup. "I'm all done."

The door opens and the overhead bell rings. I notice a blonde girl walk in. She's wearing a tan coat and a purple beret.

"Do I have time? Are you still open?" she asks desperately.

The barista looks at me, annoyed, as if it's my fault that I'm his last customer, and I laugh and shrug at him. She looks at me, pauses, then points in recognition.

"Hey," she says. "You're that guy from the Capital One commercial. The one with the hobo on the train. Right?"

The barista looks at me for a moment as he continues to clean up.

"No," he responds. "He was in that *Legal Las Vegas* episode. The one with the murdered hooker who got caught counting cards."

I look at the girl, smile, and shrug. She stares straight into my eyes then smiles back.

*

I'm walking with the blonde girl in the purple beret down Massachusetts Avenue as she sips her coffee and the gray Boston sky asperses rain as if it's holy water on our heads. It's cold, and we maneuver around the piles of snow on the sidewalk as we cross over Commonwealth Avenue toward Cambridge.

"So, what are you doing in Boston?" she asks. "Shouldn't you be in Los Angeles, enjoying the sunshine and shooting a commercial or pilot or something?"

"I had a family baptism today," I say.

"Oh—how cute."

"Yeah, I was the godfather. Not a very good one, but godfather nonetheless."

She smiles and sips her coffee, blowing some cold vapor.

"And you?" I ask.

"Oh, I'm meeting my family for a late Easter dinner," she says. "They're staying at the Hyatt in Cambridge—right over there. Probably should've shared a cab with you, rather than walk in this weather."

She points out over the Charles at the pyramid-shaped hotel on the other side.

"And I'm kind of late," she says.

We are standing in the middle of the bridge now and I look at her. She's traditionally pretty, not in the same way that Mary is—but nevertheless pretty. I smile at her and look back toward Boston.

"Listen," I say. "Do you want to come by my sister's place in Brookline after your dinner is over?"

She looks at me awkwardly.

"You want me to meet your family?"

"Not like that," I say. "Just, you know, come over for—a hot chocolate, or something."

"Hot chocolate?"

"I don't get to ask that much in Santa Monica," I laugh. "It's more like: want to meet for sushi after our yoga class?"

She blushes and laughs, then looks over at the Hyatt.

"I really have to get going. I tend to be late all the time. My family hates it."

I nod and reach my hand out to hers.

"I understand that 'hated by the family' feeling," I say. "And it was nice to walk with you."

I shake her hand and turn away, feeling the cold wind blow off the Charles and onto my face. I feel once again humiliated. *Hot chocolate? Where do you come up with something as stupid as hot chocolate? You are a comedian. You improv all the time!* I want to jump into the icy waters and baptize myself again— for the last time.

"Wait a second, Gabriel," she yells from behind me.

She runs across the crunchy snow, takes off her purple beret, and reaches in her pocket.

"Here's my card. Why don't you call me when you come back to Boston again?"

I take the card and look at her. She leans in and kisses me, chaste, on the cheek, then puts on her purple beret and skips toward the other side of the river. I watch her go and look down at the card: *Susan Wright, Substance Abuse Counselor, Massachusetts General Hospital.*

*

I make my way back to Brookline, arriving at dusk, then up my sister's snowy stone walkway. I see the Grand Marquis in the driveway, parked next to the 2009 Volvo X-90, and slowly open the front door. I walk in and remove my coat, shaking off the cold.

I walk into the living room and my father sees me. He slowly gets up and shuts off the television. I can tell that he's had a couple Budweisers.

"Put your coat back on," he says gruffly. "You're staying at our house."

"Dad, I—"

"Your sister doesn't want you here." He takes his hat from the banister and I hear him mutter, "Skipping out on your own godson's baptism. Unforgivable."

He picks up his car keys and walks past me toward the front door, opens it, then looks back. "Hopefully, she'll forgive you by Christmas."

He steps out, slamming the door behind him. I stand and look at my sister's living room for a minute, realizing that this one room is larger than my whole apartment in Santa Monica. I think of going upstairs to apologize to her. But instead, I follow my father outside into the cold.

*

I lie on my bed in my childhood room and stare at the ripped Larry Bird poster that still hangs on the wall and realize that I am truly home again. I look over at my airline ticket to LAX on the bedside table for the morning and feel the pit in my stomach, the same one that occurred each Sunday night before I had to go back to college after a long weekend home.

● ● ●

I think about not drinking anymore. I think about Susan Wright. I think about the letter I'll write to my sister apologizing, or how I will have to explain myself to my mother as we drive to Logan in the morning while she chain-smokes long Salem 100s in the Grand Marquis.

I walk to the window sill, open it, and light a cigarette, blowing the smoke into the cold air. I look out at a dilapidated tree house covered in snow, sitting silently in the giant oak, visible in the back porch floodlight. I think about how I used to spend hours out there dreaming about my future. I think about how I'll break my godson's arm if I ever see him touch a cigarette.

I hear the phone ring on my dresser and, for a moment, wish it's my Uncle James with a joke and answers to all my problems. Then I hope it's my agent, Mel, with another callback for a national commercial or a sitcom. But it's my parents' landline, not my cell. I look at the caller ID. It's my sister.

I let it ring again and look at an old Little League photo on my bureau, one of me holding a bat, with long bangs over my ears. Beside me is Uncle James, holding the new mitt he had given me for my twelfth birthday, along with a Budweiser.

"Who the hell is calling at this hour?" I hear my father yell from downstairs. I know my mother is sitting with him, smoking and doing the crossword puzzle from the *Sunday Globe*.

"It's Mary," I shout down. "I'll pick it up."

I think of what I want to say, what I need to tell somebody, maybe the most unlikely ear of all.

As I pick up the phone, I feel that everything might just be all right for the first time in a long while.

* * *

ACKNOWLEDGEMENTS

I'd like to thank the editors of the following literary magazines, who originally published stories in this collection: *Istanbul Literary Review*, *Fresh Literary Magazine*, *Coq and Bull*; and *Ekakshara*. I'd also like to thank Červená Barva Press for awarding my story, "Baptism," 2nd place in their 2009 Fiction Chapbook Contest.

ABOUT THE AUTHOR

Michael J. Atwood is a fiction writer and weekly opinion columnist for the *North Attleborough Free Press*. His work has appeared in a number of literary magazines and online journals. He is a graduate of the University of Southern California's Master of Professional Writing program, where he focused on fiction and screenwriting. As an undergraduate, Atwood studied at Boston College, majoring in English and interning for *The Boston Globe*. He now resides with his wife, Melanie, and children, William and Megan, in North Attleborough, Massachusetts, and is an English teacher at Foxborough High School. Atwood is currently working on his first novel.